LOVE and PAIN

A map of consciousness

NOTE:

The Appendix appeared in an earlier form in SPHINX Magazine,

Basel, Switzerland, Issue 33, in German translation. and later

in THE SUN Magazine, Chapel Hill, NC, Issue 85

Both copyrighted by Seed Center Books/Even Lazier, Ltd.

For information address:

Even Lazier Ltd., P.O. Box 17270, Encino, CA., 91416, USA

Library of Congress Cataloging-in-Publication Data

Despretz, Sylvain, editor/publisher.

Love and Pain ~ *A Map of Consciousness* by Thaddeus Golas

Ist Seed Center Books Edition.

p. cm

ISBN 978-0-9830574-2-0

I. Philosophy. 2. Conduct of Life 3. Metaphysics   I. Title

II. Title: Love and Pain ~ *A Map of Consciousness*

The Collected Works of Thaddeus Golas, Vol. III

I   0   9   8   7   6   5   4   3   2   I

LOVE and PAIN

A map of consciousness

by

Thaddeus S. Golas

Published and edited by
Sylvain Despretz

SEED CENTER BOOKS

SEED CENTER BOOKS

P.O. Box 17270

Encino, CA 91416

www.seedcenterbooks.com

Even Lazier Publishing, Ltd.

Love and Pain

With gratitude to
Lumin Egress, Blair & Ramona Teagarden for faithfully preserving
many printouts and letters, the late Collin Wilcox-Paxton, for providing invaluable
data about Love and Pain and other unpublished works by Thaddeus Golas,
and to Nancy Monroe, Mayor Bryan Thompson, Sarah Nelson,
the late Knox Burger, for their time and generous contributions——
finally, to Dieter Hagenbach of Basel, Switzerland, for providing the odd
missing piece of the puzzle from his vaults at Sphinx Magazine and Gaia Media.

Contents

INTRODUCTION

On a little book that [almost] never was...

Thaddeus Golas had a way about him; he got his ideas across with perfect clarity. Nearly everyone who read *The Lazy Man's Guide to Enlightenment* can tell you a story about the moment the book entered their life, and how that life was changed forever. I will share my own, since I have spent the last few years excavating and meticulously parsing through Golas's body of work—most of it unpublished—in an effort to rescue it from near-oblivion.

The '70s had drawn to a close without much fanfare, and none of our elders, journeymen and women of two mythical decades, had sounded the warning call: The magic of the 1960s' mind expanding revolution was about to vanish, leaving in its wake a world that would eventually renounce much of what had been handed-down to our young generation—simple and honest spirituality, for instance...

I was in college in 1982 when my dear friend the late Anne Day—spouse of my anthropology professor David Day—gave me the *Guide*. "You might like it," she said, coyly. The book, conveniently designed to fit into a back-pocket, has been with me ever since. The title made me laugh... The text, however, tapped into my passion for cogent metaphors and ideas, and blew my mind wide open. Thaddeus Golas was a game changer for many, and his impact on my own life reverberates today, as I find myself initiating a new publishing cycle in the work of this little known author; life can work in funny ways, sometimes.

Even though I have spent the better part of two decades designing for the film industry in Hollywood, no work I have ever done matters to me more than this present effort of caring for Golas's writing and legacy; I traveled across North America to meet his family, his old friends, lovers and wives, while collecting and editing his letters, diaries, and unfinished manuscripts. He had left a trail of writings in the care of a precious few, with the explicit hope that someone would pick up where he'd left off. He even wrote-out instructions.

When he passed away, in the spring of 1997, Thaddeus Golas had been unable to find a publisher willing to take-on his new work, despite the respectable sales record of *The Lazy Man's Guide to Enlightenment*, a book which remained in print through several editions for forty years.

Why all this trouble on my part, then? Simply put, these texts are the most important writings I have ever come across. The information they contain is priceless and unique. It is information for living. Information that is incredibly hard to come by. The effort it took Golas to articulate his philosophy reveals his immeasurable compassion— a compassion which can no longer be met with indifference and futility.

"I wrote this book to save myself the trouble of talking about it," said Thaddeus Golas in his introduction to *The Lazy Man's Guide to Enlightenment*. Because of that single line, I nearly didn't write him that first letter over two decades ago, almost missing a chance to correspond with him and pave the way for my future involvement with his work—but I did write, mercifully—and still, the *Guide* seemed a book so complete that it was hard to believe its author had more to say.

Love and Pain marks a significant evolution and somewhat of a departure from Golas's earlier work. He intended for *The Lazy Man's Guide to Enlightenment* to serve as a life raft for youths of all ages who wandered across the stormy seas of the psychedelic '60s. The book eventually became a classic spiritual manual, mostly through word of mouth, and soon sprung copycats.

By the end of the 1970s, a pop culture of self-help literature and seminars was surging, but Golas cringed at the thought of being bundled with New Age authors.

In the 1980s, popular spirituality was more in vogue than ever; it became a huge marketing scheme and began to spread its promise of frivolous rewards, quick fixes, and dominion over the physical world through positive and wishful thinking. For Thaddeus Golas, it seemed that more answers than merely 'love' were needed, if we were to find our way out of this maze.

If in *The Lazy Man's Guide to Enlightenment* he tried to show how certain things work, in *Love and Pain*, he demonstrates why many more *do not*. "Mystics ought to be more like scientists," he once quipped, "instead of wishing for science to become more mystical." He later added, "I thought *Love and Pain* might short-stop the blind submission to charismatic leaders by people who took good feelings as evidence of spirituality." For Golas, the path to enlightenment begins with absolute autonomy, and a good dose of common sense! Perhaps therein lies my own attraction to the work: it speaks to my sense of wit and logic. Golas is mystical, yet deft and lucid. He is demanding. He suffers no foolishness.

My passion for the clarity of his thinking, and for the practical understanding his work delivers, leaves me no choice but to pass on these manuscripts nearly lost in time.

A word of caution: Fans of the *The Lazy Man's Guide to Enlightenment* are often shocked when they first become acquainted with *Love and Pain*. After being handed a manuscript, on one occasion, a European businessman famously gasped: "Are you sure this the same author?" His reaction foreshadowed the book's early fate: The New Age editor at Bantam Books went further when she reportedly burst into tears upon reading Golas's new work, and promptly cancelled his publishing contract; *Love and Pain* struck a nerve. Other people who knew Golas simply walked away— people, that is, who mostly thought they'd understood him, and yet did not—for indeed, *Love and Pain* is a continuation of the work—a development of the concepts he first explored in *The Lazy Man's Guide to Enlightenment*.

With *Love and Pain*, he brings out the proverbial x-rays glasses. He steals a rare snapshot of the dark side of the moon. He shows us the blueprint of the engine that pulls the car. *Love and Pain* is deep, and powerful, but it is a demanding book. And that's a good thing!

Did any of us really expect Thaddeus Golas would come out of hiding only to repeat himself and exploit his readers by emptying an old bag of recycled tricks?

Not a chance!

Sylvain DESPRETZ
Publisher

Foreword

Why is our spiritual understanding of so little help to us as human beings?

Why do we vainly pursue magical powers?

Why do we concoct fantastic sagas of personalities surviving through the ages?

Where do evil and pain come from?

Are we doing something wrong?

Is there a way to do it right?

Is there something we need to learn to get away from here?

We have tried many answers to such questions, all rooted in the puzzle of what the spirit is and what it does. Some of the answers seem to work for a time. Some provide pleasant feelings. Some require impossible or impractical demands on human behavior. Many are pure folly, and some just whistling in the dark.

I began an answer in *The Lazy Man's Guide to Enlightenment*. *Love and Pain* is a necessary step beyond that book, and perhaps a correction to it.

The *Guide*, first published in 1972, was an emergency manual for the psychedelic era, when many were first launched into unusual mental states. In those stormy seas of subjective experience, "Love it the way it is" served as a life raft.

The *Guide*, in print continuously since publication, will still be rewarding to those who sense the consciousness with which it was written. But more must now be said about our adventures in this reality on Earth. We need an explanation for the contrast between the blissful freedom of pure consciousness and the unwelcome pain and confusion of our human lives.

In events of crisis, we do not have time for the luxury of lengthy books, nor can we rely on inspirational lectures. *Love and Pain*, like the *Guide*, is intended to suggest a few simple attitudes we can hold onto both in this life and hereafter, along with sufficient argument to give the confidence to use them. In addition, I hope to show that we can understand how we open the door to undesired experiences.

This book, like all the other writing I have done, is based on certain simple concepts. At first glance, they may appear too narrow to explain reality, but simple laws can easily build into complex systems. What we require is that the proposed laws agree with what we can see happening, and help us to understand our human predicament.

For more than thirty years I pursued these ideas, believing that if we knew how the basic units of the universe worked, we could then derive clear and specific guides for human behavior. Alas, no sooner had I thoroughly worked it out, than I began to understand that any such ideas, even the right ones, were almost useless in providing rules for behavior. To put it most simply, they were useless for the same reason that we do not need to understand quantum physics in order to fry an egg.

The basic components concern us only indirectly, even though they form our human selves. When basic entities relate to form functional systems, the systems cannot behave in a simple and unanimous way, as the components do in one-on-one relations. And the human body is a very populous system indeed, existing in a reality of unpredictable systems.

Needless to say, letting go of an effort of decades, and realizing that pain was inevitable in human life, made me a bit gloomy. Except for a couple of articles, I ceased to write and even think about it. But then it occurred to me I would have lived a different life if I had known this when I was younger.

If someone else knew about the role of pain, I would want him or her to tell me.

Since we are self-conscious systems, any practical information about systems is useful. Certainly we need any reliable ideas about the role of consciousness in our lives. I decided my concepts might be useful after all, since they lead to practical and verifiable conclusions.

The answer proposed here discards some fondly-held attitudes and ideals, but it can be relied on. It is an answer that agrees with the way the natural world actually works. When we grasp the fundamental simplicity of the universe, we will understand what we can and cannot expect from the confusions of systems. We can cease condemning ourselves and each other for failing to correct what can never be corrected. We will see certain basic rules that none of us can evade.

I have always pursued hard knowledge, knowledge that will hold up in solitude at four in the morning when the euphoria of charismatic example and uplifting lectures has evaporated. The information in this book may be hard, but it is a hardness we can rely on. It was difficult for me to accept, and I have been slow getting around to writing about it. In the end, I decided it was worth the effort to explain why, in a phrase I have often used as a reminder, "This is the necessary pain."

What we human beings need is information. No one of us alone can uncover enough of it or keep in mind all that is already known. In what follows I will try to establish that there are certain core ideas around which we can integrate a flood of details and bits of information. There are processes that will affect our fate whether we acknowledge them or not. We live in such a peculiar reality that there may be no way to do it right. But at least we can act with a better sense of confident choice, and understand what the power of the spirit really is.

ONE

The Rules

Human life is a strange madness played on a peculiar stage.

We try our best to make sense of it, to rationalize and explain it, to idealize it. We say it is an illusion, but unfortunately it is an illusion that hurts.

Half the matter in the universe is in the stars, in a continuing state of nuclear reaction, and the other half is scattered like dust in space.

It would seem that producing radiation is the preferred activity whenever material entities gather in large numbers.

We have come into being on a precarious planet, and seem blindly intent on becoming radioactive ourselves. There is no evidence in all the incredible vastness of the cosmos that there are any others like us, no evidence of consciousness that we can perceive.

How are we to understand this strangeness?

Is it true that the life and consciousness we know has arisen out of a background field that is itself not alive? That blind mechanisms have somehow given flower to organisms that can see and know? It seems to me to make more sense that the life we experience would arise from a background field that was itself alive. How would this be possible, in a way that would agree with all we know in science, and yet account for all the varieties of consciousness we human beings can experience?

The idea of atoms, as indivisible basic components of the world, has tantalized many thinkers. We owe the word "atom" to Democritus in ancient Greece. Apparently the word was too quickly bestowed on the elements, for the atoms we know are divisible. Experiment and speculation now provide a long list of names for different sub-atomic agents, a defiance of Occam's Razor: entities have been needlessly multiplied. No successful effort has yet been made to simplify quantum physics by exploring the idea that all the many named particles are merely different functional states by entities that are of one kind, or by systems of uniform entities.

That is the starting point for what is proposed here:

What if the universe is made of one kind of basic component? The true atom—a uniform, indivisible entity that is not combined from anything smaller, that exists forever. What would those entities have to be doing in order for the world we know to exist? What laws would limit their behavior?

When we contemplate the vast spaces, the fantastic energies, and the precise predictability in the cosmos above and below the human sphere, we must assume that the laws governing the functions of the basic units will be simple, indeed elegant, as we often find. For these functions are of an inexorability that will burn out, wipe out any complexity sooner or later.

Simple laws can easily build into complex systems, but complex laws would have an impossible labor to create the reliable predictions of physics and astronomy. In the same vein, a system based on equal components can readily contain the games of inequality, but a system based on inequality will inevitably self-destruct.

In 1950, I casually jotted in my journal, "Space is to energy as energy is to mass." That line set a course which ultimately led to these basic rules:

— The universe is made of one kind of entity.

— There are two states of being: expanded and contracted. (It might be more precise to say "standing momentum outward" and "standing momentum inward," but those are awkward phrases to repeat often.)

— An entity must be in one state or the other at any given instant. It may sustain either state at will.

— Expanded entities are *space*: They are permeable to each other, and can be in the "same space." They offer no impedance to each other.

— A contracted entity is *mass*. Mass entities are not permeable. They cannot occupy the same space with any others.

We might say they are "anti-space."

— Each entity may change at will from one state to the other. All *energy* is the appearance of entities when constantly changing from space to mass, mass to space, without resting in either state.

— There is only one fundamental physical interaction between entities: space propels mass. All other relations and systems are built on this interaction. (See *Appendix* for more detail.)

— Every entity thinks, feels, and acts.

— Space entities are conscious.

— Mass entities are unconscious.

— Energy entities are half conscious, since they are expanded half the time, but their consciousness occurs in billions of bits per second.

What is an entity? An entity is that basic component of the universe which may, at its own volition, be expanded and conscious, or contracted and unconscious, or alternate instantaneously between these two states.

An entity is space, it is mass, it is energy, depending on what it is doing at any given time. The functional relations between entities form all reality. They—we—are the stuff of the universe. There isn't anything else. When an entity is expanded, it *is* space. When contracted, it *is* mass. When alternating rapidly between space and mass, it *is* energy.

It is not possible to hold up a single entity and say, "This is what it looks like." We cannot see subatomic particles, and we cannot isolate one space entity from another. We are currently puzzled by energy's wave-particle duality, but that is easily explained in terms of this concept: An energy entity is a particle half the time; when it is perceived as a wave, it includes both the expanded and the contracted states, the space and mass of its alternations.

All that is proposed here is that we assume that the universe has this fundamental simplicity of components: a single kind of entity, and see where the notion leads.

We human beings are self-conscious systems, made of entities who are mass most of the time, energy some of the time, and space some of the time. We have a mental self-consciousness that is formed of the behavior and participation of billions of individual entities.

All entities experience feelings. They feel pleasure, love, when their behavior is identical to that of neighboring entities; they feel pain and related unpleasant emotions when there is a functional difference between themselves and others. (Energy's potential for persistent pain will be explained later.)

One barrier to grasping that all entities are capable of consciousness is that we cannot recognize behavior as being conscious unless we experience it as conscious when we do it ourselves.

If a subatomic particle was conscious some of the time, how could we tell? Of course, since recent discoveries in genetics, and since the development of the microchip, we can allow that a great deal of information can be stored in a small space. How big is an idea?

We have all been in the free consciousness of space, all of us: every entity in every atom of our bodies and brains. And we will be there again. Nothing can take away from us our essential nature. Nothing we do as human beings can affect our fundamental freedom. What is conscious in us, what is unconscious in us, will always exist in our essential selves.

Each individual entity has absolute freedom to be conscious, to be unconscious, or to alternate at will between these states. A relation between individual entities is immediate and total. Consciousness always pushes away unconsciousness. Though there can be no such binding requirement as perfection in the formation of the universe, as far as we can conceive of such a quality, the laws of the universe are perfect.

How do these simple and perfect laws result in the difficult and confusing world we human beings live in? That is what we will explore.

TWO

Reality and Pain

What is reality?

Reality is any set of functional relations between the basic individual entities. Oddly, we might say that each entity exists but is not real, because it is unique, whole, and is not a set of relations. And reality always happens, but does not exist, because any specific reality can change or vanish when the components behave differently.

Does consciousness create reality and rule it?

The answer is No.

The significant word is "functional." Each entity's choice of function is to be expanded or contracted or to alternate between these states at will. Being expanded and conscious is one and the same, therefore being conscious is only part of any entity's potential action. We could say consciousness is a participant/observer of some of what is happening. Any realities, any sets of functional relations, are always something of a mystery to consciousness.

The mystery is not noticed in space or mass relations, because those entities who are continuously conscious or unconscious are not aware of "others" at all. There is no functional variation in environments of absolute space or absolute mass.

But in any realities involving energy entities, not only are mysterious others perceived, but there is also the high probability of pain.

Pain is of such crucial importance to us that I am enduring the pain and effort of writing this book to explain it, and must risk the reader's pain and boredom as well.

In addition to being described as a functional difference in proximity, pain can also be defined as impeded momentum. (Unfortunately, the transfer of information between us human beings is not entirely unimpeded.) When an entity's actions agree with neighbors, the sensation is one of unimpeded momentum, of pleasure. When there is a difference in actions, the sensation is one of stopped or slowed motion, of pain.

The absolutes of space or mass, continuous consciousness or unconsciousness, are always richly pleasurable in feeling.

Energy relations, however, can easily be painful, because rapid vibrating introduces another sort of behavioral difference: being out of synchronization. One vibrating entity may be expanded whenever its neighbor is contracted, and vice versa, repeatedly. Each is always aware of an unconscious neighbor who is painful to be near, and who does not move away. Let us dwell on this situation, because it is the key to all the undesired feelings in the universe, including those in our human lives.

Energy is the devil, the tease, the thrill, the delinquent, the messenger who delivers only half the message, the marker of time.

Energy promises dominion over the world. It accumulates endless details of information. It creates forms and systems and destroys them. It has beginnings and endings, monotonously repeating changes, and therefore time belongs to energy relations.

It is the outside agitator. It has unforeseen side-effects. It is explosive and excessive, and there is never enough of it.

Throughout much of the universe, energy entities avoid pain by being instantly agreeable, duplicating any move, any vibrational pattern near them. Usually this instant agreeability is enough to minimize pain. (We human beings trade on this agreeability for our computer systems, radio, television, and other electronic marvels.)

However, in a reality of material/energy systems like those on Earth, pain is not so easily avoided.

Pain is simple: it is what entities and systems feel when they are near others behaving differently. Pain is not a problem for basic entities, because any single entity at any time may leave a painful relation by changing its behavior. We can easily understand, however, that when individuals gather in numbers in a group, the behavior of the *group* is not likely to be immediate and total in relations with other groups. There are certain groups, like atoms, which persist as functioning systems for great lengths of time, even though individuals may leave and others join the system. These atomic systems, as we know, join with other atoms to form chemical systems, and those in turn can relate to others in organic combinations: cells, plants, and animals—self-duplicating systems.

To survive, such systems must endure pain longer than the differing neighbors, or try to move away, or drive the other away, or build up insulating mass, or compromise, or destroy what is perceived as the source of the pain. Pain generally happens as a persisting condition only in rare circumstances such as those on our planet, where we find material/energy systems encountering other systems and contending with varying vibrations of energy.

Even so, most of the organisms on Earth do not find pain a particular problem, since they function without much memory or anticipation, and over the eons evolved as a compromise with the environment and other organisms.

The human system is cursed with pain because it is a self-conscious system.

Space entities, with their profound consciousness, rarely encounter realities like ours, but we human beings, as self-conscious systems, are obliged to be aware of occasions of pain. Consciousness does not solve the problem of pain; only changes in behavior or location can alter a painful condition. Feelings have two variables: function and distance. The closer together two systems are, the more intense the feelings.

The complex oddity known as the human brain has evolved self-consciousness. We are conscious, but as systems we do not have the free motion of basic entities when they are conscious. We cannot change rapidly enough to alleviate pain, and in any case we would disintegrate physically if we did so. When we are too agreeable, our systems fall apart.

Our bodies and minds can be said to be sets of statistical probability, behavioral choices by billions of autonomous entities in chemical and cellular systems. These components of our bodies must reliably repeat whatever they are doing, and must not react to pain by changing to agree with outsiders. To do so is to "contract a disease."

Since we are self-conscious, we are obliged to be aware of pains, both physical and emotional, over which we have little or no control. What is worse, these pains must be endured and dealt with in order to maintain our physical and mental integrity.

The corresponding fact of our Earthly reality is that we must avoid or moderate pleasure. Pleasure is by definition a behavioral agreement with others. If a system's components alter their actions for the pleasure of agreeing with outsiders, the system suffers what we call a failure of immunity. If we are too agreeable in our social behavior, if we always choose to avoid pain, if we indulge in excessive pleasures, even innocent pleasures, we will find our bodies and minds disintegrating.

The "punishment" of overindulgence is not in some future hell, but here in our human lives. There is no spiritual virtue in enduring pain and avoiding excessive pleasure: these are necessary and useful purely for the survival of our human selves.

If any system is to last, its members must be loyal and must reliably perform their roles. If the members change what they are doing, the system changes or dissolves. Once a system grows as large as the human body, there is a great deal of redundancy, and it can lose many millions of entities a day (and gather in others) without being affected significantly. There can be some variation in the behavior of the components without changing the nature of the system. Probably none of the atoms in our bodies is the same from one year to the next, so there are not many entities, if any, who stay around for a lifetime. As mentioned earlier, each of us is a statistical probability.

The important point is that the laws for basic entities are not often useful or relevant when we consider the relations between systems, because each system involves an obligation for persistent, reliable, and repetitive functioning, a sacrifice of freedom of action. The majority of components at any given time, whether basic entities or sub-systems, must be consistent in behavior in order for a system to continue and survive. They must endure the pain of acting differently from their neighbors.

It is this fact that is the key to all the madness and confusion and pain, the laboriousness of human life. The basic laws of the universe, the inviolable freedom of each entity, these are useless to us, because systems cannot behave as simply and freely as the basic individuals do.

It is a rule that none of us can evade: it is necessary that we endure pain and effort in order to survive. We have skated over this unpleasant fact with vain hopes and unreal memories, but in every moment of human reality we must deal with it. We argue with the necessity of pain in a thousand ways. We wrongly assume that pain is unjust, that we should always attempt to save ourselves and others from any twinge of pain or difficulty.

No one deliberately formed these systems, these human beings. No one gave us consciousness. No one can solve our problems, or evade the laws of reality for our benefit. The very idea of rescue is self-defeating: if we were freed from pain, our systems would not last long.

It is only as self-conscious material systems that we suffer. None of the basic entities forming the atoms in our bodies is in any discomfort: each entity is free to leave at any time, and many of them do leave or move around. From the fundamental point of view, there is nothing that needs to be done about life on Earth, and indeed there is nothing that can be done. Meditate as long as we will, open ourselves to space consciousness as we may, we are complicated self-conscious systems bound to this local reality.

We still have freedom of consciousness, to think what we will.

If our ideas contradict the laws of functional relations, however, the laws always prevail.

Even the highest consciousness cannot contradict the law.

No one can bring this local reality to a "higher" state.

Relations between systems will always be confused and unpredictable, defined by pain and rotted by pleasure. We live in a lunatic local reality which has nothing to do with our spiritual future. In a space reality, pleasure is profound and pain is impossible.

THREE

The Spirit

Let us now look beyond our local reality.

Suppose it is true that all space consists of conscious entities?

We may then assume that space would be continuously conscious, and energy/matter systems partially so, depending on time-lengths in an expanded state.

What is it like to be space-conscious? Is it something we human beings can experience? What would be the probable experience of the conscious individual entity?

Space feels no pain. Pain is a functional difference in proximity, and space entities are free to move anywhere they wish. The momentum of space entities is absolutely unimpeded. They push away any contracted beings. And since pleasure, love, is a functional agreement in proximity, space entities experience profound ecstasy and calm in permeating each other.

There is so little matter in the universe in relation to its expanse that most space entities go through all time without ever encountering any matter, much less becoming involved in a human life. Our experience on Earth is just as strange to "spirits" as theirs is to us.

For instance, space entities need not be careful of what they think, since their ideas have no functional consequences. They are free to think anything they wish. They need not think only good thoughts because good and evil are irrelevant: no undesired experience can be forced on a space being. They need not even be concerned with what is true or factual. They are absolutely free to think any concept at all, and every concept is experienced profoundly. It is not possible for any entity to control the subjective consciousness of another.

Size is not a factor, since space beings can move through each other, and have no structure to maintain.

There is no history to recall, no need to remember who thought what and when, no details of any significance, no store of information to be retained. All concepts are equally available to all entities.

A space being experiences a feeling of infinite power because each does have unlimited power to determine its own position, thoughts, and relations with others. This freedom does not require any control of others. It does not require conforming to any concepts of others. No quantity of any kind is needed, not size or numbers of entities. No energy is needed, certainly, because energy is a more limited condition than space.

The momentum of space is twice the speed of light. (Light is energy, and energy is expanded only half the time.)

Space propels mass: space pushes away material and energy entities during the time-periods those entities are contracted, but that propulsion is uniform. It is not added to or subtracted from. When we expand and stay conscious continuously, we merely join the uniform propulsion that already exists. No space entity has more or less power than any other space entity.

Yet the subjective sense of each is one of enormous power, luxury, understanding, and dominion.

Space time is always Now. There is no concern with a past or future. Entities have no beginning or end, no development, no growth, no learning, no training. They are complete as they are, possessing all the power and knowledge they need, since they always control their own thoughts, relations, and location.

If by chance or curiosity a space being should become aware of what is happening on Earth, it would assume that the human reality was just another set of concepts, illusions that could be changed at will. And this is precisely the message that many human mystics bring back from temporary space excursions. Many people pursue the erroneous notion that reality can be directly controlled by thoughts and imagination, but space rules do not apply in a material reality.

The fact is that space beings are not repositories of virtuous platitudes about human existence. Their sense of understanding is deep, but they do not possess information about the endless details of energy/matter interactions. They have no need of such information. They would find it impossible to believe that human beings are having undesired pains and emotions. They do not feel what we feel.

In more familiar words, the gods do not understand our human values because they are not behaving and feeling as we do. Certain people who have had mystical flights come back with the notion that humanity also can live a completely value-free existence, with no regard to good or evil consequences: for instance, Aleister Crowley's "Do what thou wilt shall be the whole of the Law." This is a serious mistake, since human behavior does have good and evil effects. Human beings can have mystical illuminations that are euphorically convincing, but that are misinformed about Earthly life.

Space beings readily and cheerfully duplicate the concepts of others, therefore anything we think in a mystical state is instantly and magnificently amplified. For example, if you think of yourself as an unworthy sinner, then that is what you feel, magnified, with ecstasy. Perhaps the ecstasy will give you the idea you have been forgiven, and of course you will be extravagantly and deliciously forgiven. What you think is what you get.

We may understand our human mentality better, and explain our tendencies to enthusiastic error, if we take the time to consider what consciousness must be in a state of pure space. Space consciousness is so different that we are likely to judge it as hallucination when we briefly encounter it. It is so empty of memory and anticipation, so complete in a sublimely confident trust, with no need to choose for the future, for what happens next, that we might even regard it as no consciousness at all: a sublime void.

Consciousness and unconsciousness are the two basic innate states of being for every entity in the universe. Every entity must be either conscious or unconscious at any given instant. The choice is absolute: the only way we can be "partially" conscious is over a period of time, changing from one state to the other, as energy does and as we do when we are being energy.

No entity can be deprived of consciousness—it is not contingent on anything outside the self. Distinct from our energetic mental activity, the experience of pure consciousness is out of context, one of the aspects making it strange to us when we open to it.

As an innate state, consciousness is not dependent on perceptions. Indeed, since perception is the experience of differences, a characteristic of energy, space entities do not have perceptions at all. They know whatever they wish to know, as a concept that they create and are one with. What they know is not experienced as outside themselves at all. Should they physically find themselves briefly in the vicinity of energy or mass, they will experience themselves as "one" with that also.

Although the only real force in the universe is that space propels mass, this does not give consciousness the power to control energy and mass in any specific way. The propulsion is uniform and identical everywhere—it is what we now think of as the force of gravity. Space merely pushes away any contracted entities. Mass moves toward other mass because that is always the direction in which there is less space, less propulsion. The more mass entities are pushed together, the more intense the pressure, not because space is pushing harder, but merely because there is no counter-propulsion at the center of a gathering of mass.

A space entity's sense of self is profound and absolute, even when it is participating in a conceptual flow involving many billions of other space beings. The sense of oneness is total at all times that consciousness is continuous. There is no awareness of any "others" to control or manipulate or govern, and of course there is never any sense of being governed by others.

All feelings are specific to functional relations between entities. The behavioral agreement of space entities is continuous and unvarying. They offer no resistance to each other, and the sense of profound love and pleasure is constant.

A space entity cannot comprehend the feelings of energy/matter because it is not behaving as energy/matter does. A space entity passing through this planet would be aware of the local feelings only as ideas: beautiful, richly pleasurable sadness, beautiful pain, beautiful longing, beautiful ugliness, beautiful destruction, beautiful emptiness and boredom. These words rightly suggest to us the sublimity of great art, for artists do take the risk of opening themselves to profound consciousness, and then accomplish the extremely difficult task of translating those experiences into a material communication, so that other people are reminded of how it feels to be fully conscious.

It often happens that prolonged consciousness is not helpful or practical in human life. Out of it comes great art, religion, and science, but it is not a stable state for the person who is blessed or cursed with it. As human beings we must give priority to concepts that are relevant to our local reality, to the survival of our human systems. We may let our minds and feelings wander, but we must always exercise caution when we act overtly.

It is convenient to think of space as "spiritual," but mass and energy are equally spiritual. People have felt free to say anything about space consciousness. It is a sort of no-man's-land: nothing can be proved or disproved about it.

Often when human beings do become briefly aware of space consciousness, they populate the void with imaginary hierarchies, legislative systems, architectural wonders, divine plans, and so on, none of which have any substance except as ideas.

Whenever we venture into pure knowing, all definitions and words are useless. That is why all discussions about telepathy and the like are pointless: none of these exercises of consciousness is reliable in the complex energies and unconscious masses of the human context. How would one differentiate between precognition and telekinesis? Random telepathic communications may occur, but who would depend on them? We have enough difficulty understanding each other in clearly written and spoken words.

Space consciousness can *know* of past events and highly probable futures because space is not bound by time (time belongs to energy-level phenomena), but space does not *feel* those events as we human beings do. Also, the events are usually known out of context, without a human sense of significance.

We must understand that prolonged consciousness is an *action* of being continuously expanded—no vibrating—and cannot be achieved by any method of ideas or energetic behavior.

What we must do is simply will to be conscious:

"No matter what happens, I am conscious all the time," and repeat this intention, with or without such words, until we actually do it. However, if we do so, we must be prepared for an experience that is often alien to the human mentality, and irrelevant to human reality. The ecstasy of full consciousness does not fit easily in human life: the local rules, the functions and feelings are different for us human beings.

There is no single entity that is *the* consciousness of a human mind. Our mental consciousness is the mutual formation of billions of material/energy entities, each of whom is conscious for little bits of time. There is no single entity that is the soul or spirit. When it comes to that, all entities are spirits. There is only one kind of entity that forms the universe, and there is nothing else.

FOUR

The Mind

It is often said that we are using only a small part of the mind's capacity, and many of us have shown that the brain is an exceptional system. But we also give the mind too much credit for having the power to make changes, to do it right. Even great minds and well-intentioned souls have made blind errors.

Since we are conscious to a degree, we are certain that we are something other than our bodies, yet we can give little credibility to any experience away from the body.

As human beings we feel a constant need to manipulate and control matter and energy for our survival and comfort. When we imagine a God, we imagine a vast intelligence that also wishes to manipulate and control, to create and destroy. But what if God is not large, but very small, perhaps even sizeless? And what if there are an infinite number of such entities, who have no intentions about energy and matter at all, since energy and matter are those same gods functioning differently?

Since neither God nor gods will alter our destiny, we must do it for ourselves, insofar as it can be done, with our human minds. Surely we have enough examples of human behavior by now to isolate some essential rules. Let us acknowledge that our consciousness resents being involved in systems at all, let us set aside what we would prefer to believe, and see at last the reality.

Consciousness of itself does not cause anything specific to happen other than steadily pushing away unconsciousness. Thought does not do anything. Energy entities, picking up an idea with their partial awareness, will always express the idea in a vibrational form. Whatever cannot be communicated in this way does not get communicated by energy, as we are learning in our efforts to create artificial intelligence with computers.

Energy, in turn, may manipulate matter (usually by its agitating effects in local relations) into various forms and processes in attempted obedience to an idea, but the results are often distorted and at best require constant repair and upkeep.

It is an irony that stupidity and error are actually a proof of human consciousness: if we all acted as precisely as computers, as energy acts, there would be no way to tell that another human being was conscious. When we demonstrate intelligence or stupidity we are showing that we are conscious.

Consciousness as we know it with our human minds is a flow of perceptions, stored information, comparisons of perceptions, editing for relevant perceptions, always in a context in which our responses and actions make a difference in physical experience.

We are constantly obliged to be aware of information about other physical events if our system is to survive.

It makes an enormous difference whether what we think is true or false. Economy of attention demands that we focus on what is pertinent, but it is easy to guess wrong. What may be a relevant fact at one time may be false information in another context.

In addition to what we might call housekeeping perceptions, we can of course use our minds for concepts not relevant to our physical context: fantasy, intellectual flights, logic and reasoning, imagination in general. We often keep ourselves happy or motivated with ideas of no immediate relevance to our current situation, as we routinely perform the chores of daily life. Anticipations and memories keep our minds busy while the system functions on automatic. These ideas are so important to us that we may resent it when events force us to deal with immediate, ongoing processes. Paying attention is often a burden.

Consciousness is still consciousness, however abbreviated in durations or however involved with a human system. But our mental consciousness does not have the deep pleasure of space because our functions are not as easy. We do not have the conceptual freedom of space either: usually it is only with dedicated attention or, less reliably, with psychedelic substances that we can will to take our attention away from our local reality and its systems, its time-patterns, and its complicated context.

All entities are equal, but obviously all systems are not equal. All human beings have minds that are capable of some consciousness, but not all minds are equally efficient. In fact, a person with an inadequate mind, with deficient information, may know profound consciousness and even produce great art and display saintly insight, while another with a highly efficient brain might be narrow in consciousness and empathy. There is no correlation between a brain's efficiency and consciousness.

The brain is a material/energy system: it is likely to be uneasy or unstable when relating to space consciousness. When we will to be fully conscious all the time, we may find we are going beyond the boundaries a brain can accommodate, that our bodies are suddenly swept with terror or depression to keep our attention down to Earth. If we truly wish to be fully conscious, we must risk a sense of dying or going mad: some who have taken the leap have not come back to tell about it. It is utterly wrong to think of higher consciousness as some sort of benign psychotherapy, or a way of living an idealized or powerful human existence, or a demonstration of superior human conduct.

Throughout history we have erroneously believed "powers that be" of one sort or another were responsible for events on Earth. We might lose faith that there were any higher beings at all, but cannot believe there might be higher beings with no such "powers" and no interest in events on Earth. We prefer to believe we must be fascinating to the gods if they exist.

Space consciousness is not going to solve human problems. "Higher" consciousness is not a storehouse of better data, of precise details about material/energy interactions, of ways to choose and control events, of proper ways to behave as a human being. Space consciousness will not cure disease or stop wars or eliminate mental malfunctioning or prevent crime.

Space beings did not form the Earth or the complex organic systems that have grown up on it. There is no divine intention for human life. The only solution that a space entity could realistically propose for us is that all the billions of entities being matter and energy should become space, should stop vibrating, stop being mass and energy, so that the whole planet would disappear. If most of the entities forming the Earth prolonged their conscious states OR their unconscious states, the planet would vanish. Since this is not likely to happen, neither for the planet nor for our bodies, our human mental consciousness goes on, no matter how often individual entities leave and others arrive, no matter how often our minds open to the wonderful bliss of space consciousness, and no matter how we try to escape our perceptions with drink and drugs.

Consciousness does not operate by the same rules as the mind. If anything, the mind is an impediment to realizing profound consciousness. We do not need the brain for consciousness. If space consciousness is our goal, we must be ready to leave the brain behind, along with all else in this Earthly reality. The human mind is a marvel of intricate energy, but is not a greater wonder than pure consciousness. We should not expect our minds to perform miracles that even pure consciousness cannot achieve.

F I V E

Arguing with the Universe

It is not correct to say that individual entities are governed by laws, since the laws grow out of the freedom of each individual being.

Each unique entity is absolutely free to determine its own experience: to be conscious or unconscious, or to vibrate freely, and to think what it wills.

It is this freedom of elementary action that cannot be violated, that defines what the laws are. This freedom establishes the priority of causation for all that happens.

Some relations are those we call subatomic and atomic. These relations are voluntary, formed only by what the basic entities are willing and able to do.

Building on these basic choices, systems like molecules and chemical compounds are formed, but are limited by what their elements are willing and able to do.

Cells can form only within what molecules will do. Larger life systems, in turn, are dependent on the behavior of cells and other microorganisms.

When we encounter this priority of causation, we give it various names: inert matter, hard reality, the laws of physics, or the mysteries of nature. We assume that these events are devoid of consciousness and volition, but our human perception is showing us only the operation of the law. The behavioral probability of billions of entities in action appears to us as "mindless" since its range does not arbitrarily change. An aerial view of a city's traffic will look similarly mindless, though each driver is conscious and has an intention.

Nothing in our sciences is contradicted by the suggestion that all entities are conscious when expanded, and are conscious part of the time when vibrating. Indeed, some recent puzzles in physics could thus be solved with a simple explanation.

We usually think of "realism" as the acceptance of obstinate processes that do not yield to our will and desire. But what we are dealing with is a simple priority of causation based on the freedom of each entity. This priority can be expressed as laws. The laws of physics are the same for all entities in the universe, at all times.

Reality is just the working of the laws. Since the entire universe is composed of relations between entities, all of it is real, and there is no such condition as being outside reality or exempt from the laws. The sense of reality in space consciousness is profound, so much so that I am always tempted to spell it with a capital R when I refer to it.

Space is real. Energy is real. Mass is real. None of it is illusory. All is formed of the equal beings that are the universe. When we are space we are not obliged to be aware of matter, but that subjective experience does not mean the human world is an illusion or that it can vanish from reality.

It is true that consciousness has no limits in what it may conceive of. What we may think and dream is not limited by laws because consciousness is innate in each of us, not dependent on relations with others. There is no law over consciousness itself, no limit on the freedom of thought.

Consciousness is absolutely free, and even we human beings can think concepts contradictory to reality. However, reality is immune to ideas contrary to the laws of behavior. If we attempt to carry into action what the law forbids, we will fail inexorably.

We human beings do a great deal of what we might call "arguing with the universe." We admire reputed magicians and other entertainers who offer the promise of evading the laws that govern reality. This is a strange state of mind: trying to prove the spirit exists by contradicting laws presumed to be ordained by the spirit.

Changing one's state of health by a boost in morale or by determined effort is an energy phenomenon, not an intervention of supernatural beings.

If we are going to be grateful for anything, we ought to be grateful for the certainty of the laws of the universe. The fact that a law impedes our intentions does not mean the law is wrong, or that our supposed spiritual powers are confounded. It means that we human beings are creating a problem by trying to contradict or manipulate the free behavior of other entities. We blithely challenge and defy reality's obvious patterns, and then when we find ourselves in trouble we appeal to the heavens to alter the laws for our benefit.

Because we can manipulate energy and matter with some conscious intention, we erroneously imagine that the universe was similarly manipulated into existence by a larger intelligence. In fact it would be impossible to form a cosmos in that way, and it is not necessary to make such assumptions. Given the existence of unique and equal entities behaving as they verifiably do, all other phenomena may occur as a matter of probability.

No grand plans are required or possible. Space propels mass uniformly: all variations in our physical world result from the time-lengths of voluntary contraction by unique entities, visible as energy and matter.

Given the absolute priority of causation outlined above, no additional laws are necessary beyond the rules for one-to-one functional relations between entities. (See Appendix.) The universe is thus exquisitely simple in design, as near to being no design at all as possible. It is unlikely there is any more complicated way a construct as vast as the cosmos could continue. Our security and certainty rests on simple laws, the behavior of simple elementary timeless beings just like ourselves.

On the other hand, as human beings we may easily be confused and puzzled because systems-relations are often insane or perverse from the viewpoint of the fundamentals. As one person to another, as one group of people to another group, we can certainly behave in ways which the law forbids in the relations of individual entities.

There is a gulf between our human mentality and consciousness at a basic level. It would never occur to a space entity to try to rule other beings. A space entity can certainly know there are others, and can conceive of relations of all kinds, but it feels itself to be one with whatever it is aware of. A fully conscious being has no mechanism to influence the behavior of others apart from the transmission of ideas, with of course no way to enforce the priority of one idea over another.

But when contracted entities gather, pain and the threat of pain becomes an implement. The unique entity can end a painful relation instantly by changing its own behavior; a system like the human body does not have that flexibility. If we want the pleasure and power of participating in a system, we must endure the liabilities. There is no way any material system can be "more spiritual" than any other system. Being conscious, being a spirit, will take us out of human reality, but it will never give us control of physical events.

Because of the pain of functional differences between material systems, people can harm others and be harmed, both intentionally and unintentionally. We can dominate each other. We can manipulate, injure, benefit and destroy. We can be stronger in a group than alone. We can use force and fear and violence to impose unwilling agreement. We can lie and mislead. We can use pleasure as a bait for destruction and theft. Some success in these actions leads us to make the mistake of thinking that reality in general is subject to our willful intentions.

The behavior of self-conscious material systems is as near to a contradiction as the law will allow. The law is not being violated, because the freedom of the basic entities is not impeded. Human life is a good example of the chaos that would reign in the universe at large if one entity could in fact dominate another: the absolute freedom of each basic entity is thus a necessary assumption, because the cosmos would otherwise be very different.

As human systems, we cannot be completely space, we cannot be completely mass, we cannot be completely energy—we are always a mixture of billions of entities in various conditions of vibration or stasis. We can force other systems to bend to our will, but we can never intrude on the freedom of the individual entities. To our regret, we have seen what happens when our manipulations disturb the internal stability of atoms.

We have the self-interest of systems: we want to keep our bodies alive and to reproduce them. These evolved obsessions have the highest priority in our passions and behavior, for we are the consequence of eons of evolution from other systems that had the same priority. To the extent that we vary from it, we are judged to be mad or frivolous.

The general human experience cannot be elevated past these concerns. The apparent first law of every system is to maintain itself. Of course, if it does not observe this priority, it does not continue as a system.

The self-conscious human system grew out of probabilities and is maintained by them. The choices we can make for our human experience are bound by probabilities. There are so many variables in even the simplest physical event that any question of conscious mental control of reality itself is ludicrous. We have had so little understanding of reality that the purest intentions of the purest minds have led to a magnified capacity for destroying our species. We have mistaken the manipulation of probabilities for an ability to control.

We delude ourselves by our small successes as we move back and forth on the surface of our irregular sphere.

We are an intrusion of consciousness into a material context. We attempt to use our consciousness for purposes for which it is not equipped. Consciousness of itself is a pleasure, a mastery, a dominion over experience: it has no need of elaborate bodily systems, no need of manipulation, no need to be concerned with survival or reproduction. Attempting to control physical reality is not the proper role of the spirit.

This book itself is the result of my bafflement as a consciousness in being obliged to maintain a physical self.

On occasions when I achieve a free-floating awareness with no identity, here on Earth or elsewhere, I feel much more at home. Reaching this understanding about material systems satisfies me as a consciousness because I am no longer trapped into trying to fix the unfixable. I am no longer arguing with the universe.

I do not blame God or humankind for our predicament. We just happen to be participating in a peculiar local distortion of reality. While I am human, I will honor the laws that make this experience necessary.

I am writing for the benefit of other consciousness, should any wish to gain some understanding of what we can and cannot do.

Just as individual entities define reality by their actions, even though the behavior of any single one may seem insignificant, so also each human being helps to define our social reality by his or her behavior.

Every person who understands the necessity for enduring pain and effort makes a difference in the human reality. It may be a pointless difference in the light of eternity, it may even be useless in the context of a given culture, but it will make a difference. It makes an immediate difference to the person who chooses to behave with some restraint, because that person will have different feelings. And there may in time be a ripple effect, so that the social reality will be different also.

In time, too, humanity at large may cease to argue with reality.

SIX

What Is Love?

Love is the pleasure of the universe.

All feelings are variations of love or the absence of it. Love is any agreement of action between entities or systems.

Love is available anywhere in the universe, high or low, wherever entities agree in their behavior.

Pain, both physical and emotional, occurs wherever there is a difference of behavior.

Love is not a property of either consciousness or unconsciousness alone, but of perfect identity in behavior. That perfect identity is difficult to maintain in relations involving energy because of its never-ceasing variable vibrations.

Following the star of love will not necessarily lead us upward to full consciousness and freedom from pain. If we make the pleasure of love our priority, it can fix us where we are, or even lead us into more confusion.

Love is a measure of our relations with others. The love we feel is formed by our own behavior and the actions of others, not by our ideas or intentions. To love another perfectly is to experience a oneness so complete that there is no sense of another. A perfect agreement of action can be sustained only by entities who are continuously conscious or continuously unconscious; in energy realities love is always temporary and mixed with pain. Since we human beings live in a material/energy reality, the occurrence of pain is frequent and common, and enduring it is necessary for our survival.

Therefore love is not the universal answer to all our problems, since material systems must maintain their differences from other systems.

The thought is grand and poetic that all the unbounded vastness of space is conscious, profoundly loving, and free of pain. But it is false to try to ennoble our human condition with the reassurance that we are of one kind with space entities.

Cosmic space is an infinite number of different entities conceptualizing whatever they wish to be aware of. In order to feel what they are feeling, we must do what they are doing: we must sustain continuous expansion and consciousness.

All agreements of action are equally pleasurable. In this respect, there is no standard of value by which to judge realities or states of consciousness. We can be happy anywhere in the universe or unhappy anywhere, depending on whether or not we agree readily with the behavior of those around us.

We must always choose which others we wish to relate to. A choice to move to a different state of consciousness will place us in disagreement with those we now love. Transitions are exciting but painful. On the other hand, if we automatically choose to avoid pain and to take whatever love is easiest and nearest, we will not move out of our present reality.

The laws of our relations are simple and fair. All functions demonstrate them. There is no such thing as an unlawful function or feeling: the laws cannot be contradicted.

In any experience of love in or beyond this human reality, if we are still perceiving another as apart from ourselves, then we are being energy, not absolute space. This is true no matter how glorious, sacred, or overwhelmingly loving that other appears to be.

Energy's experience of love is sensational, sometimes so excruciatingly delicious that it is impossible to dwell in it for any length of time. If a peak is followed by a valley of loss, then what we are having is an energy experience. Matter's experience of love is generally an agreement of unconsciousness, empty of knowing. From the perspective of energy, matter's pleasures look disordered or rigid. Energy entities flatter themselves that they are showing love for matter by trying to change its form and behavior into a pattern that energy finds agreeable.

Human beings can of course have feelings of love for each other and achieve agreements of behavior that feel pleasurable for a time, a temporary sense of oneness. But sustaining even these limited feelings of love is difficult because we are distinct systems.

All feelings have two factors: function and distance. We come close to others for the reward of love and pleasure, but at short distances the pain of any behavioral difference is greater also. In human relations, we often experience the greatest pain in relating to those we love the most, since there are inescapable frictions in our reality which cannot be eliminated.

Perfect functional agreement is not possible between human beings, and we should not expect perfect love from each other. No one person alone is responsible for the pain of a relation. The pain is in the difference in the behavior of two people, not in the actions of either one alone.

Feelings never lie. Emotions always tell us exactly the degree of our agreement or disagreement with others. If we suppress our feelings because we prefer our ideas about what is happening or what we think should be happening, to that extent we will probably encounter more pain.

Perception is the experience of differences in function. The more we perceive, the less pleasure we feel. The more intense the perception, the more painful it is.

Agreements can be felt and known, but cannot be perceived, which is why they often feel insubstantial. A perfect functional agreement is invisible. Love and good feelings grow with agreement: the better we feel and the more we know, the less we perceive. "Love is blind."

To love consciousness, we must be space. To love energy, we must not only be energy, we must be synchronized energy. To love mass, we must be unconscious. Love is an absolute identity of action with our neighbors.

Our energy reality is pervaded by the frequent probability of non-love, or pain. There is no higher or lower value of energy. All rapidly alternating entities are energy, and suffer the same liability of potentially unsynchronized vibrations, of persistent pain.

The oneness of space is not a mystically difficult state to achieve. All an entity needs to do is to cease vibrating: to will to be continuously conscious. Energy imagines a mysterious power that knows all and controls all. But space has no interest in the information that energy wants, and has no desire to engage in energy's passion for gaining agreement by manipulating others.

Is love the power? No.

Consciousness is the power. But it is not the power to do anything specific. It is the power to push away from itself all unconsciousness, to remove itself from all energy and mass entities. Consciousness is not the power to control the material world: it is the absolute power to be free of it.

When we are continuously conscious, we will feel a profound love, so rich that it is incredible to human mentality. But we cannot reach it by setting love as the only goal. If we wish to move back to space consciousness, we must disagree with our current material reality: we must be "unloving" or indifferent.

When we do choose to be continuously conscious, we awaken where we have been sleeping. That is, in the proportion of time when we are unconscious, we are propelled to the vicinity of others equally unconscious, and when we open to continuous consciousness again, we then awaken to the perhaps dismal thoughts around us, as well as the pain of being newly different from our neighbors. If we cannot endure this unpleasantness, and retreat from consciousness to feel the pleasure of human agreement, to feel love now, then we will remain in this Earthly reality.

In human life, love must always encounter pain, because the differences between nations, races, cultures and individuals are real. Highly conscious people have told us to love others as we love ourselves. We all recognize this as wonderful advice, and we all know it is impossible to follow while living a normal life. As self-conscious systems, we must maintain a degree of difference from others in order to survive.

It is neither possible nor desirable to eliminate all our differences. Laws based on pious wishes will fail. Understanding the roots of pain, perhaps we may control the urge to kill, the instant gratification of violence. Good manners may be our best hope.

To love whatever we encounter will give us relief and frequent pleasure, but we will have no reliable character or consistent relationships with anyone. We become what we agree with and love. Therefore, we must choose to love what we wish to become. We must behave now as that which we wish to be. To reach the existence we want, we must behave the same as those entities who now enjoy that existence. Each of us has the responsibility of choosing the kind of love we wish to know, the reality in which we wish to live, the other beings with whom we wish to relate.

Love is truly a blessing, and can happen in any reality, but we should not expect love to do what it cannot do, and certainly should not expect love to happen where it cannot happen.

A perfect love is not possible in our imperfect human reality.

Love is universal because it can happen anywhere, but love is not a means to take us to higher consciousness and the life of the spirit. Love is always profoundly wonderful, but it is not the answer, the power, or the means for our deliverance.

SEVEN

Governing Ourselves

Considering the thousands of generations of experience of this planet human beings have had, it is time we worked out better ground rules for Earthly existence.

We must solve our human problems where we are with what we have. We will not take these bodies and minds to heaven: we go to space as pure consciousness and nothing else. Space entities are not sending forth rules, regulations, or moral lessons: few of them even know we are here. Our reality is as much an unknown to them as theirs is to us. We are here as the result of an unlikely sequence of probabilities. The rules we need to observe were not capriciously invented, but come from the laws that apply to all beings.

The universe exists by virtue of the freedom and self-government of every entity in it.

All government begins with self-government.

Every basic entity governs its own actions. No unique entity does anything wrong because it cannot do anything wrong: it always finds itself relating in time to others behaving exactly the same way. This happens because space propels every entity while it is contracted, and eventually it moves close to others having the same time-lengths of contraction. What we see in any reality is ourselves: others essentially behaving as we are.

The human body and its brain were not built up as an intelligent or planned project in the Earthly environment. We were formed out of blind impulse, a joining to push forth anything that might work, using anything already persisting. Just as we do in our technology, systems take the line of greatest success and least resistance: they do what works, what repeats, what can be realized, even if it is stupid. That is the way the body and brain evolved.

Consciousness did not plan our reality, and it cannot tell us how to govern ourselves. Consciousness is limited in dealing with contraction of any kind, the more so when mass and energy form operating systems.

It is not merely that others think or act different that makes vibrating mysterious. No entity can be conscious of its own unconsciousness, since these are opposite states. It therefore cannot understand any vibrating. (It is only the persistent behavior of those around us that tells us in time what we ourselves are doing when we vibrate.)

Consciousness cannot control when and how others vibrate. Consequently it has no mechanism for regulating the behavior of others, and could not form our systems or rule them.

Perception is an energy phenomenon, a vibrational feedback. We perceive because of time-periods of contraction in ourselves and others. We can have information about the material world, and we can perceive it, but we can never be fully conscious of it.

The faster we change states and the more energetic we are, the less continuity of consciousness we have. As energy, we are half-conscious in billions of tiny bits per second that run together, like seeing a film. We could say it is impossible to act and to know fully at the same time: even in our human actions we do not govern every event in our bodies when we decide to walk across a room.

All human behavior will forever be tantalizing to consciousness.

For these very reasons the kind of information I am trying to deliver is hard to come by, and hard to describe. We are energetic systems, and must govern ourselves by feel and by experience. We often find that consciousness is not of much help.

In a state of space, every entity can govern absolutely the content of its awareness. By contrast, energy invokes a flood of feelings and perceptions uncontrolled by our choice of ideas. Energy reality is a variety of behavior by billions of entities and is beyond knowing or control by the consciousness of any entity or group of entities.

The only way we can know how we are vibrating, as unique entities or as human beings, is by our feelings. There is an absolute coincidence of specific feelings with specific actions and relations. When I tried to chart these correspondences, I soon realized it was hopeless: I would have to walk around pinning labels on events as they were happening. However, here is a short list of indicators:

When we are functioning as space, continuously expanded and conscious, our experience is that of complete oneness with all we are aware of, with feelings of sublime euphoria, love, serenity, and profound passion, with no perception of any pain or instability. Since we are equal entities, all conceptions of any kind are equally available to every entity.

We are energy if we perceive other entities in any way, as phenomena that we are not causing, as sources of feelings that we did not choose or do not wish to continue, and if our feelings have an edge of tension about what might happen next, intense sensations that feel temporary or uncontrolled; if we feel overwhelmed by magnificent phenomena, by events that seem to be happening faster than we can understand them; if there are flashes of intense pleasure or pain, tingles of danger, hierarchies of power, and on and on to all the phenomena of our human world.

When we are functioning as low energy or matter, being in a contracted and unconscious state for the greater proportion of any time-span, we are dimly conscious, feeling dull aches but no sharp pain; we find it more pleasurable to be unaware, to ignore whatever is happening, like a sleep rippled by slow dreams.

Beyond this, our experience within any context is always determined absolutely by behavior, not by ideas or information. In our human reality, feelings are never caused by the behavior of one person alone. Our feelings and sensations are always a complex recipe of mingling vibrations.

There are no simple answers to the human dilemma.

Often we find that a small solution that can be repeated is more useful than a grandiose remedy, since a small problem that recurs is a large problem. Also the simplest route to changing our feelings is to change our own behavior or location, not the behavior of others.

Greater consciousness is of little help in our situation, though it is certainly useful in providing detachment from energy's confusions.

What is needed, however, if we wish to be involved in human life, is self-management, an orchestration of behavior. It is destructive to pursue unlimited pleasure. We need not seek out pain, since we will encounter enough of it in the normal course of events. We need to teach and practice a balance of pleasure and pain, of love and rejection.

What we can do is study systems and gather accurate information about how to maintain them. Every pleasure must be weighed: How much disintegration is it likely to cause? What self-discipline, postponing of gratification, must we adopt to make a pleasure allowable?

While it is probably impossible for any information to keep pace with energy's changes, such analysis would be better than our self-defeating search for external causes of damage. We condemn viruses, germs, alcohol, chemicals, drugs, weapons, foreign ideologies, tobacco, cults, sunlight, and sex. We try to regulate a host of variables, including the speed limit. It would make more sense to be alert to the key to all disintegration, which is excessive pleasure, instant gratification, the flight from pain.

If people do not regulate themselves, no other regulation is effective. It is legitimate to remove from society those who will not or cannot control themselves. Who should be allowed to define our social reality, the murderer or the useful citizen?

We can, if we wish, ignore the way reality works and fill our minds with thoughts we find more congenial. The mind coordinates information, and we are free to create a warm feeling by feeding misinformation into it. But reality will happen according to its rules, regardless of what we think about it.

The rules are not invented or intentional, and are not designed to annoy and hurt us. Every entity has autonomy, and the rule is that when entities do not agree in their behavior, they feel pain. If this were not true, the entire universe would be as confused as human life on this planet. Our human systems are built of hosts of entities who endure pain rather than exist as agreeable non-systems. The rules do as much to discourage the formation of a reality like ours as can be done. If entities prefer the excitement and pain of energy systems to the sweet surcease of space, no one can forbid them the choice.

Humankind exists because of the behavior of billions on billions of entities over whom there is no control of any kind beyond the pain that already punishes discord.

We are systems, and we must observe the limits, the imperatives, and the self-interest of systems, both personally and socially. It is not much help to remind ourselves that it would feel better to be somewhere else in the cosmos, since, as human beings, we are not able to go there. We cannot apply the unconditional love in space reality to the human social reality.

The implicit suggestion of a book like this one is that we can govern ourselves intelligently. However, the variables of our human world are largely unconscious or half-conscious, and our intelligence must deal with what is not intelligent. Our consciousness must deal with what is unknowing. Our feelings must encompass what is unloving and painful.

Since it is impossible to have enough information about every conceivable set of relations, we try to form summarizing principles to help us steer through the torrents and backwaters of human behavior.

A spectator-consciousness may feel sublimely confident, but when we enter the field we learn that practice, training, and established customs count for more than inspired impulses. On the human field of play, we are always and ever obliged to make realistic choices.

We are the components: what kind of social organism do we wish to create? Who will define the reality?

How are we to govern ourselves in human reality with our own behavioral choices?

If we maintain continuous consciousness, we will arrive at some sublime insights, but we will be more and more removed from other people.

If we choose the oblivion of unconsciousness, of sleep or drugs, we are likewise removed from human relations. Obviously, the choice for most of us is to lead an energetic life, to play energy's fascinating games. But if we want energy's power and glory, we must pay the price of enduring energy's disorder and pain.

Just as in the universe at large, the only government that will work in the long run is a government that trusts the individual.

Each of us must be responsible for his or her own self-government...

E I G H T

Power

The only absolute power in the universe is the power of space to propel mass, of consciousness to push away unconsciousness.

It is not an optional power: a continuously conscious entity cannot abdicate from it. It is a uniform power: no entity has more of it than another. Space entities never move any energy or mass to do anything specific. The forms and systems of our world are determined by time-lengths of contraction by energy and mass. In that sense, we might say that our physical world is a subtraction or retreat from consciousness.

When an entity chooses to be continuously conscious, its power to be undisturbed by energy or mass is absolute. It is aware only of the feeling of agreement with other space entities, a feeling of profound and cosmic love, as well as whatever concepts it wishes to think of.

Naturally, if there are a lot of energy entities around, as there are on Earth, there will also be narrow feelings and ideas evident to space entities because of energy's half-time bits of consciousness. However, a space entity can easily move away from here or, to say it better, experience this Earth as a quickly-vanishing illusion.

The real power of consciousness is the power to repel all manipulations, all the complex interactions of vibrating entities, all unconsciousness of whatever order. Even in our human sphere, we can retire from active life to contemplate, to meditate and prolong our consciousness. We can also will to maintain continuous consciousness regardless of our involvements—the reminder I have used is, "No matter what happens, I am conscious all the time."

Consciousness is the power to be free of energy and mass, of pain and unconsciousness, but it is never the power to manipulate, to impose order of any kind, to govern, to create or destroy material realities.

While an entity is continuously expanded, it cannot feel what energy and mass are feeling. Its power over this world is the power only of absolute detachment. In short, while we are in any way participating in being human, we are not being fully conscious. So long as we are active in Earthly reality we will experience sensational and uncomfortable emotions.

It is impossible for an entity to be in two states at once. This is the impossibility that energy appears to be trying to achieve, to be space and mass simultaneously, to relate to both space and mass. If an entity chooses to act as energy, its time-lengths of consciousness are bits that approach the vanishing point. As soon as any entity wills to manipulate others energetically, or to be ruled by others, it diminishes its own consciousness. Storing information, memory, and repeating vibrational patterns are energy's substitutes for knowing. Energy's billions of bits of consciousness are subjectively experienced as a continuity, but they are empty of the resonance of sustained consciousness.

In a context like that of our planet, energy's activity can produce specific effects in the behavior of matter. It is this manipulation that energy thinks of as power. But such power is specific, local, quantitative, temporary, and is contingent on the contracted state of matter.

Power in a reality like ours is of course energy's idea of power: achieving the pleasure of agreement by enforcing it on others with the threat or imposition of greater pain. Energy is easily manipulated, and sees the world in terms of manipulation.

Power for a living system must be, primarily, the power to maintain itself and duplicate itself. Since we will always encounter the varying behavior of energy and other systems, pain is inevitable. To exercise the power to survive, therefore, a system like the human body must, as a first requirement, deal with pain without itself changing. Even for a headache, I remind myself: "Power is the willingness to endure pain without changing your system." (It is my fond hope that my cells will get the message.)

Energy's power games are so common in human relations that it is important for us to understand their root in feelings. The goal of both dominance and submission is simply the pleasure of agreement; it is not always correct to impute evil or hostile motives. The will to power is essentially pleasure-seeking, and like any pleasure it can be a threat to systems.

In our reality, energy's changes must constantly be dealt with, and the rate of change is a significant factor. A system can compromise gradually with changes that would be destructive if occurring too quickly. In the old phrase, seduction is preferable to rape.

The process of pleasure that is most dangerous is instant gratification. By insisting on it, people damage themselves and also do damage to those around them. We blame "the system," we blame the state, we blame the indifference of the strong, but each person has a potential worst enemy within the self: yielding to the urge for instant gratification, immediate agreement, the avoidance of the slightest pain. The will to power has these same intentions.

However, no system can survive intact unless it is willing to endure pain. By the same token, fortitude bestows genuine power, sometimes enormous power, even for one individual who is willing to outlast the endurance of others. Often in history we have seen governments brought down by a single person willing to endure the pain of being different. (Naturally, as this becomes general knowledge, the stakes will escalate.)

But the truly powerful are not bullies. We live in a quantitative reality and can marshal great force, but the capacity to inflict pain and destruction is useless without the willingness to endure pain oneself. Energy's power is as transient as energy itself. If humanity understands that the pleasure of agreement is the true goal, and can be achieved in gentler ways, perhaps we will leave off our delusions of power and our violent rage for meaningless victories.

We think of power as the ability to control energy, matter, and their systems and processes. In the universe at large, consciousness does not participate in these actions. As self-conscious organisms, we have the advantages and the penalties of an unusual experience: a conscious pursuit of power over others.

Is consciousness related therefore to what we recognize as spiritual power? No, not by virtue of the content of anyone's ideas, since any power is a physical process. The force of gravity depends on the amount of mass, and in a social parallel anyone's expansion reduces the amount of mass and thereby the weight of others. It is thus more than a metaphor to say that a social group will feel lighter when any of its members has a high consciousness.

Of course, too much lightness of spirit in time produces uneasiness. It threatens to unravel social systems as any pleasure does, and highly conscious people have often been imprisoned "to preserve order." Bursts of spiritual revival are likely to be followed by painful hangovers of reintegration.

The messages of charismatic leaders are often turned into operational systems by energetic disciples, and then solidified as institutions and worshiped as unalterable writ by the mass-minded.

Energy-minded people are constantly jockeying for position to see who will have the power to define an ongoing reality. They adjust their own behavior or attempt to influence the behavior of others in order to reach agreements. They also frequently object to the inertia of the masses. Often this objection is disguised as benevolent concern, a passion for social justice, or a concern for morality.

Largely unconscious people, the mass-minded, exert the power of mute resistance, non-responsiveness, refusing to agree with the busyness of energy. But they can be agitated and heated up by energetic people.

Space-minded people recommend consciousness as a solution to human problems, the energy-minded propose energetic solutions and new systems, and the mass-minded try to impose limits on thinking and action. Essentially we are all trying to achieve agreements that will enhance our pleasure and survival. Our actions are motivated by feelings and expectations of feelings.

The exercise of Earthly powers is delusive, a costly and consuming way to gain the pleasure of an agreement from others, but it is an endeavor that preoccupies us all in one way or another.

NINE

Feelings

People sometimes say that the bliss of heaven would be boring. Human feelings up and down the scale of pleasure and pain certainly seem to make for an interesting world. Particularly so, since feelings cannot be reliably created or controlled.

No recipe for a feeling is foolproof: an action that is rewarding at one time is painful at another. The circumstances are never quite the same.

Yet if feelings are so fascinating, why is it that so large a proportion of the human race muddles its senses with alcohol and drugs? We prefer vicarious experiences more often than not, in films and books and television.

We love to feel, but find reality unwieldy all too often when we try to act out a scenario of our own. Can feelings ever be understood?

We live in a feeling universe.

Some of the universe is conscious, some is unconscious, some is energetic, but ALL the universe is suffused with feelings. Feelings are determined by functions, by behavior. Since there is nowhere in the universe where there are not individual entities relating to each other, there is nowhere in the universe where feelings do not occur.

It is the rule that identical actions in proximity are experienced as pleasure, or love. Correspondingly, differing functions in proximity are experienced as pain, or discordant emotions.

Most of the entities in the universe are space, in continuous functional agreement, and therefore in a constant state of profound pleasure and love.

Mass entities that are continuously unconscious also feel no pain in their relations with each other.

All the subtle variations between these absolutes are produced by relations between beings who are not consistently conscious or unconscious: by energy.

Since each entity may alter its vibrations at any time, no relation between energy entities is predictable with certainty. That means that no feelings between energy entities are completely predictable.

After the experience of roller-coaster extremes of sensation, many energy entities are no doubt grateful for the monotony of instant adjustment to the vibrations of others.

Human feelings are a complicated problem because they are formed by tides of activity by a great number of entities in each human system. Because pain is so likely and frequent, we often choose whatever opportunity we have to escape it, to enjoy what relief and pleasure we can. Within any system, pleasure is allowable as long as the components do not perform damaging actions, and as long as they are always ready to endure the pain necessary to maintain the system when the occasion calls for it.

Moral and ethical codes serve the practical purpose of imposing some restraint on gratifications. Since our modern industrial systems make survival easier for us, a wider variation in personal behavior is permissible. Reasonable people even call for the lifting of legal prohibition of pleasures that "do not harm others," but pleasure and agreeability are always a threat to any system. It no longer works to ascribe moral codes to divine authority. Moderation would appear to be the answer, but that is extremely difficult to legislate.

It is not the availability of pornography or drugs that is dangerous, but our failure to understand that unlimited pleasure is not possible for us without the consequence of disintegration for both the person and the society. In recent decades, both heterosexuals and homosexuals were caught up in the belief that unlimited sexual pleasure could be enjoyed. The consequence was disintegration, and not merely from diseases like herpes and AIDS. When pleasure of any kind is indiscriminately pursued, the individual personality suffers disorientation and confusion. It is vain to try to base a social system on a type of pleasure.

We always pay for pleasure, with restraint beforehand or with disintegration and pain afterward. It was practical perception that led earlier cultures to evolve restrictive codes of behavior. In the individual instance, as a relief from work and discipline, reasonable pleasure-seeking cannot be faulted. But there are always some who foolishly believe they can enjoy perpetual pleasure without paying the dues of maintaining their own bodies and the social and economic system.

Systems evolved as a relief from pain. Like all of energy's busyness, this is a useless evasion, as it turns out, because the peculiar result is that our systems must always live in a context of pain. There is no energy system in which unlimited pleasure is possible. Our moral and ethical choices have no reference to the divine or to any afterlife. They are choices that must be made to determine as far as we can the kind of community in which we wish to live, and the kind of mental and physical nature we wish to maintain as individuals.

If we allow pleasure-seekers to define our social reality, we will live in a disordered social system. It is even more foolish then to blame "the system" for the condition of derelicts and criminals. Every reformed addict or alcoholic knows the price in pain that must be paid to reestablish physical integrity. Sentiments of pity must fall before common sense if we wish to live in a decent society. Surely we have been self-conscious as a species long enough to recognize common sense and act on it.

Space is carefree, but we as self-conscious systems cannot be carefree. We must avoid threats to survival. In other words, we must regulate momentum in many ways, and limit our love and agreement with others. We cannot always opt for the most pleasant and permissive feeling.

It is difficult and stressful to make such decisions often. The practical solution is to join in a social complex in which our behavior can be automatic and habitual. To let our behavior happen then without conscious governance is a kind of unimpeded momentum, which is to say pleasure and love.

Nevertheless we must always be watchful and critical of the social groups to which we give our loyalty. Rational organizations can be taken over by destructive leaders. Many battles of feelings are fought under the banners of political ideas or religious beliefs, notions which have no real substance.

It is time to take a hard look at our indulgence in the gratifications of violence. Tens of millions of healthy human beings have been slaughtered in the 20th Century. The difference between this century and earlier ones is not that we are more chauvinistic or racist, but that technology has given us the means to destroy each other more quickly and efficiently. Technology has magnified the consequences of our unreasoning passions a millionfold.

We cannot escape undesired feelings in our reality. Feelings can be changed or modified only by a change in behavior, not by taking refuge in idealistic hopes and expectations. No matter how many supposed enemies we destroy, no matter how we reorganize our social or economic systems, we will always encounter pain. We must learn how to use our pain before our flight from pain destroys us.

TEN

Is Pain Necessary?

It is important for us to understand what is and is not necessary in the universe as a whole.

It is necessary for an entity to be either space or mass at any given instant.

But it is not necessary for any entity to change states rapidly: it is not necessary, that is, for any entity to be energy.

Therefore persistent pain is not necessary for any basic entity. This is in fact good news, since we can be certain that when we leave this reality we will not have to go through eternity contending with pain!

Any energy entity can escape pain most simply by ceasing to vibrate, by sustaining its conscious or its unconscious state.

To be energy, to vibrate rapidly, is the first mistake, because energy systems always have the potential for unsynchronized vibrations, persistent pain.

We human beings strenuously object to the fact that pain occurs at all, and we tend to look for its causes and remedies outside ourselves. Even when we look within, as in psychotherapy, we search for events in which we were in some way injured in the past.

The true remedy for pain would be to cease our involvement with energy. That is the only permanent relief from pain. Alas, since we are such elaborate organisms, we do not have the option of effecting this escape. We are obliged to live with the frequent probability of pain. Worse still, we are conscious of it. To a free consciousness, the attempt to maintain energy systems is madness. Our human sort of consciousness is fortunately extremely rare in the universe.

When we find we cannot escape pain, many of us muddle our nervous systems or seek the help of medical science. The staggering figures on consumption of tranquilizers, painkillers, energy-boosters, and other drugs and drink, the human costs of useless surgery and other medical intrusions, need no detailing here.

Yet a rigid avoidance of pleasure is not a practical attitude either.

The question is: How we are to deal with the obvious lunacy that love and agreement can harm systems, and rejection and disagreement preserve them? It is this unfortunate fact that brings our ideals crashing to earth.

We might take a clue from organisms themselves, and employ the flexibility of fluids to lubricate friction. We might yield like water in our social interactions. Our bodies are largely water; perhaps our behavior should be equally flexible.

In analyzing methods of dealing with pain, we can speak only in terms of general probabilities. Even the most faithful obedience to rules is no guarantee of survival, since the context around any system or species may change, and our adaptations may become useless.

But at least we can understand what it is that happens, given a consistent context, when a system disintegrates.

Plainly stated, the root of disintegration is a change in behavior by any of a system's components.

This change may occur on any level of subsystems: within the atom, the chemical compound, the molecule, the cell, the organ. Similarly, a society is affected by the behavior of individual people and social groups.

The change may occur when a stranger or maverick friend threatens pain or promises pleasure, and our components agree with inappropriate behavior for either reason. Unfortunately, of course, we do not control the behavior of our bodily components. At best we may manipulate probabilities to survive.

However, those probabilities are based on certainties.

It is certain that systems will experience pain in relations with other systems, and with vibrating entities in general.

For human beings, pain is necessary.

It is also certain that a change in behavior by the components of a system may damage or change the system. The altered behavior may occur either to enjoy more pleasure or to nullify pain.

The system has the option of expelling and replacing the changed components, or of compensating for their role by depending on other components to maintain the operations required.

No doubt the greatest disruption in our bodies occurs, not from an initial invasion, but from a change the rest of the body cannot yet perceive as inimical, for example when a cell is co-opted by a virus. It is hard for the immune system to treat a cell as an enemy when it still feels like a friend.

Our bodies may also react as though enemies have power when they have none, producing shock reactions, often more damaging than an actual injury or enemy. An illness or chronic pain may be the body relating to a stimulus that isn't there any more. The most dangerous enemy is one who provokes us into harming ourselves with sudden moves and overreactions.

Our bodies exist in the first place because there were groups of entities who tried and are still trying to avoid pain by joining in systems. Through trial-and-error, a system may seem to offer a solution, but the good feelings of "belonging" are often temporary. The burden of maintaining the system always follows.

Matter forms into more and more elaborate organisms when agitated by painful relations with energy, beginning with photosynthesis on the planet's surface or by chemosynthesis near volcanic rifts on the ocean floor. But that solution creates systems in a context in which pain will always occur. Our human bodies are a stage in this process. The stimulation of energy that provoked us into reality then becomes a condition of survival. Thus, for our organisms, pain is necessary.

Pain is so much associated with injury that we may find it difficult to grasp that we are damaged, not by the painful phase, but when we try to end the pain by yielding, by agreeing with alien behavior, or by changing our homeostasis to deal with the threat of pain. That is, when parts of our bodies initiate behavior that is counter-survival.

We tend not to judge pleasurable changes as threatening, and therefore pleasure can often damage us more than pain.

It is not the pain or pleasure that "causes" damage, but our system's response to them.

If we were able to convince our cells to remain loyal, to act without change, to endure pain longer than the aliens or to let pleasure fade away, our bodies would suffer little harm. Obviously such fortitude is unlikely, since we cannot control our billions of cells, but it is an understanding we can use in our social relations. We can also benefit by modifying our futile effort to nullify every slight pain or discomfort with drugs and other remedies.

The probabilities of our reality are based on certainties with which we cannot argue, and from which spirituality will not save us. For human beings, pain is necessary.

ELEVEN

The Uses of Pain

Pain is the boundary marker between systems and forms of behavior. Our reaction to pain determines the kind of reality we live in.

Because we human beings are self-conscious and have memory, we have many ideas about pain, and often these ideas are wrong. Confusion is inevitable, because systems do not interact simply. Nevertheless, the tides of change in systems are brought about by the behavior of their simpler components.

It may help clarify our thinking about pain to understand that painful conditions are always a conflict between entities that are equal.

The intensity of pain is the same for all the contending entities.

The main variable is time: the entity or system that endures the pain for a longer time without changing will continue as it is. The one who gives in will change, or move away if possible.

The essential of survival power is thus the willingness to endure pain for a longer time than others, even if it is only a split second longer. Of course we cannot consciously control the behavior of the atoms, molecules and cells in our bodies, but in our human behavior there are many times when we can mold our identities by letting pleasure pass and by holding fast when confronted by pain or difficulty. We can also use this information to avoid complicating our lives with an endless flight from pain.

It is not the painful event that scars us. Whether we are damaged or not depends on our response. If we endure without changing, we will emerge feeling stronger and better defined. But if we alter ourselves to nullify the pain or to feel love, the change will be incorporated, and our character will show effects from the experience. Also, we can be as readily molded by pleasure, by willing agreements in the absence of any pain.

Pain of itself is not a punishment. Pain is not necessarily a signal that we are doing something wrong, or that we have failed in some attitude or technique for feeling wonderful. Pain is not necessarily a sign that one person is being oppressed or deprived by another. Any sort of difference in culture, class, or style can be uncomfortable. Good manners are a way of easing such frictions.

Many societies have learned the uses of pain. Various tribal cultures have initiation rites: disorienting isolation, physical injury, or trials of hallucinatory plants, mystification and terror. The resulting sense of power, maturity and identity is real, for the initiate gains definition. The rites are a genuine passage to adulthood. Even the milder initiations of fraternities and sororities form a useful sense of social identity.

By the same token, when we use punishing pain to modify or control behavior, it will work only if the other persons give in. If they endure the pain without changing, they emerge feeling stronger, clearly defined, and confirmed in what they were doing. Torture victims and martyrs may die, but if they do not yield they die with a sense of power and conviction. Elaine Pagels suggested that the display of ecstasy by dying Christian martyrs worked to convert the Romans to Christianity.

Therefore it is chancy to try to use force as a social control: force may just as easily give strength and definition to the criminal. Inflicting pain does not inevitably produce a desired consequence. The key is the unpredictable response to pain: agreement or disagreement, acquiescence or resistance.

We cannot adjust ourselves, especially in psychotherapy, by trying to isolate events that "caused" damage in the past. Instead, we should revise our attitudes to pleasure and pain, so that our future behavior will be integrative and strengthening.

We cannot expect that human life will ever be continuously ideal and pain-free.

It is probable that many of the emotionally disturbed are in their predicament because they have already indulged in too much gratification, or have overreacted to pain, and they may engage in therapy as an additional avoidance of pain. If the therapist's goals are the same, the process cannot succeed.

Most advice-givers commit a disservice by promising a rosy future, when in fact there is always a price to pay. Euphoric predictions may stir an audience, but the real result is that people feel even more inadequate when they fail to realize the promised uplift. Unrealistic pretty pictures make an unpleasant reality all the more vivid.

In current American culture, we have gone beyond producing and using necessities of survival. We have become a consumer society, indulging and amplifying the very action of getting. We buy anything at all, even rocks that we could have picked up from the ground ourselves. We pay exorbitant interest for the instant gratification provided by credit cards. We are acting on the assumption that pleasure should never be delayed, that no one should feel pain for any reason, emotional or otherwise. In our "pursuit of happiness," we have come to believe that happiness and pleasure are synonymous.

Many members of the healing and social-service professions come from the middle classes, and react to people from different classes or cultures—especially the less-prosperous—by assuming that those people are in pain. What in fact is painful is the difference in social behavior patterns. The lack of money is incidental to behavior; the possession of money will not result in behavior more agreeable to the middle classes, no more than public education has produced a nation of intellectuals.

There is no system of social or economic justice that will take the pain out of life. White males have always treated other white males just as cruelly as they have treated any who are not white males. The basic well-meaning error of socialist theory is that we can form an economic system that is painless for the weak by inhibiting the strong.

The rise of capitalism has been linked to roots in the moral rigors of Calvinism. We can indeed see the rise of

Protestant religions as a rejection of the indulgences, in all senses of the word, of European cultures and the Catholic Church of earlier times. Yet in recent times we have become so much a consumer culture that Catholicism is currently criticized for requiring too much restraint on pleasure.

If we are to understand the development of our minds, our bodies, and our social and economic systems, we must analyze the ways in which we modify our behavior in relation to pain, the expectation of pain, and in pursuit of pleasure.

In the ceaseless agitations of Earthly life, painful events will often be arbitrary and apparently unjust. Pain will always be a fundamental of human life, and there is no social system or choice of behavior that will avoid it.

But we do have the option to make use of the processes of pain to form the reality we wish to live in and to become the kind of persons we wish to be.

T W E L V E

Energy

Energy is tricky to understand. It is not the opposite of space or mass. It is not the opposite of consciousness or unconsciousness. Energy has no opposite: it is itself a rapid alternation of opposite states, space and mass, by the basic entities. Each energy entity can voluntarily cease to vibrate whenever it chooses to do so.

From the viewpoint of space, energy displays some consciousness, but its time-length of consciousness is almost zero in any given instant, and space cannot merge pleasurably with it.

The subjective sensation of the energy entity is one of absolutely unimpeded momentum, the pleasure of its constant motion in changing states. But it must instantly synchronize its behavior with any vibration in its neighbors to avoid pain. It always lives with the potential of causing pain and being vulnerable to pain.

Energy is never as conscious as space nor as unconscious as mass. Energy knows something, but it knows without feeling deeply. Energy carries information but it has no sustained knowledge. It has intense sensations but no wealth of feeling. It is all changes, but its repeated changes are monotonous. It offers itself as a slave so willingly that it obsesses our attention, and its limitations become ours.

Energy is full of thrills and makes startling displays, but the thrills may suddenly turn painful and the displays may vanish mysteriously. It reliably transmits details as long as the information is phrased in vibrational form, but it has little understanding of the messages it carries.

Energy has no sustained subjective states, neither conscious nor unconscious, even though it experiences its bits of consciousness as uninterrupted. Since it cannot credit subjectivity, having none of its own, and since it knows only what it can perceive, energy expects that all information will be objective. Among human beings, the energy-minded insist that information be susceptible to proof, available to perception.

During the years I spent persistently thinking through this concept, it was energy that eluded my understanding the longest. When I wrote *The Lazy Man's Guide to Enlightenment*, I knew that my comprehension of energy was incomplete, and I slid over my mentions of it. I even made the error of speaking of rapid vibrations as a high state of consciousness. Afterwards I tried theorizing that perhaps it was possible for an entity to be partially expanded and partially contracted at the same time. Until the puzzle was solved, this concept could not be correlated with what was already known to be true in physics.

The breakthrough came years later and, as is often the case, seems blindingly simple now. The answer is that every entity must be either expanded or contracted at any given time. It can change freely from one state to the other, but it cannot be in both states at the same time.

It is the familiar 0 and 1 of computer language.

When these insights into energy first burst upon my mind, I was for a time certain that it was energy's probability of pain that made it the villain in our drama. Then I came to understand that most of the energy entities in the universe do not suffer because they are so ready to agree with each other.

Our human systems-reality is a complex mixture of consciousness and unconsciousness and energy.

There are no cosmic villains.

We must, however, clarify the role that energy has in our local reality in order to understand our value judgments of good and evil.

Evil, of course, is whatever threatens our systems, but it is the very existence of our bodies in the first place that makes possible the consciousness of pain and the experience of events as "evil." When systems evolve that require energy, then those systems can feel pain, can disintegrate, and can judge events as good and evil. There are no cosmic reservoirs of good and evil. Such judgments are totally irrelevant to the unique basic entities at large in the universe. In other words, totally irrelevant to our "spiritual future."

It is an irony that Genesis represents the knowledge of good and evil as an attribute of the divine, when it is precisely this "knowledge" that is of no concern to the gods. We can allow that the Eden story is one of many attempts to rationalize the lunacy of human reality. We might characterize energy itself as the serpent's apple, for it does introduce the experience of good and evil. But we might just as easily blame consciousness, for it is the self-consciousness of the human animal that turns our paradise into hell. Consciousness does not belong in this proximity to energy and matter, and normally would not be sustained in this context.

Energy's virtue and its failing is that it is obliged by pain to be instantly agreeable to the behavior of its neighbors. We can see in an elementary physics text the illustration of erratic waveforms as entities try to duplicate several different waveforms at the same time. Energy duplicates desirable and undesirable events with equal indifference.

We might speculate that, because energy is itself a combination of opposites, it always delivers good and evil in equal degree, indifferently and unavoidably.

The comedy of human efforts to make energy show a profit of benefit is endless. We spend hours a day in cars commuting, so that we may "live" in the country. We were told that high-tech firms were "clean" industries, and then found that ground water was polluted with chemicals. In the early 1950's we were assured that a cupful of matter would provide the atomic energy to light a city cheaply, and since then we have seen billions spent on monstrous structures in the uncertain endeavor to make atomic power safe.

Each of us must decide whether energy's fascination is worth its pain.

At least we should be aware that it is not the only game in town, that we can prolong consciousness to detach ourselves and, in time, leave this sphere.

The simple will to prolong our consciousness can also give a temporary taste of our cosmic context in space. That knowledge alone might be enough to keep us from taking this planet too seriously. Perhaps we linger for the unusual experience of failing and making a mess of things.

Whatever our choice of behavior, we must understand that energy will never provide a reliable solution for anything.

THIRTEEN

Can Energy Be Managed?

Science is information about energy. Energy is the volatile agent in our human reality, both in our own behavior and in the world around us.

The humanities are a parable of consciousness: ideas that are timeless and unchanging, beauty that is always fresh, wisdom and love always profound.

But whatever our selection of ideas and information, we as human beings must begin by acknowledging that reality is formed by behavior, by functional relations.

The essential problem we face as human beings is the channeling of energy, focusing it, insulating to keep it in and to keep it out, moderating it so that our continuity systems are enhanced rather than destroyed.

Science is our agency for managing energy. It is not the single path to knowledge, but our human consciousness must recognize the reality of variable functions.

Energy produces effects and feelings that consciousness can never know fully. Entities can know each other as space, or know about each other as energy and matter.

Can Energy Be Managed?

Space entities do not need to manage energy, or to understand it, though they are of course free to know that energy happens, that energy is the autonomous behavior of others like themselves.

It is our human consciousness that needs science, information that we often find less than inspiring.

All relations between entities obey the law that space propels mass. Energy's effects are produced by its bits of propulsion alternating with bits of being propelled, in various frequencies and patterns of alternation.

The weakness, error, vulnerability, or failure of energy systems is not a flaw in the basic entities. Energy fails precisely because all entities are equally powerful in governing their own experience, and it is impossible to maintain the enforced agreement that energy seeks.

Pain persists because energy systems maintain a proximity of space-mass relations that would not otherwise persist.

Energy has abdicated from the power of a steady state, being neither space nor mass continuously. A rapidly vibrating entity in fact removes itself from its power to govern its feelings. Energy is a subtraction from what we are. It is as close as an entity can get to being nothing. Energy is weak, not strong. It achieves a sense of power by inflicting pain on others.

Energy is ignorant, not knowing. It prides itself on the endless details of information which it radiates through other energy entities.

Energy achieves pleasure only by constantly fleeing pain, by perpetual adjustments of its vibrations, and by this same process transfers bits of information.

Energy produces the experience of measurable time, since there is no demarcation of time unless entities change states. In the human reality, we measure time with vibrations and other repetitive phenomena. Energy never has enough time because it is only a bit of time before it changes to an opposite state. The continuity that we know even as human beings depends on the steady states of space and mass, of our consciousness and unconsciousness.

Energy's continuity is endless repetition, repeating cycles of change. It is monotonous until it is explosive. It perpetually strives to achieve goals and then must abandon any desired state in order to agree with the next vibration it encounters.

Energy is reliable insofar as it vibrates constantly, but it is unreliable in its readiness to change, to agree with any new pattern that comes along.

We must always be cautious and attentive in manipulating energy, including our energetic human selves. Unrestrained expressions of energy are obviously not an automatic good. Very often the solution to a problem is the application of less energy, not more. Not every problem needs the intervention of our busy management.

If we limit our attention to the behavior of energy alone, then we dwell in a world of banality and equivocation. Even for scientists themselves, the preferred emotional state is the excitement of uncovering new data, or in teaching those to whom the information is new. It is doubtful that many people reread a physics text for recreation or delight. Indeed, it is essential to scientific information that subjective emotional preferences be set aside.

It would be helpful if subjectively-minded people ceased asking science to lend its hard-won authority to ideas that have nothing to do with energy.

It is something of a tiresome necessity, but it is a necessity that we accommodate ourselves to energy's reality in order to manage it.

Energy is not only tiresome but dangerous, since it may vary its monotonous repetitions suddenly and un-predictably.

We already have this tiger by the tail, and it is a very large tiger indeed.

FOURTEEN

A Conversation

ENERGY *s*ays: It will stop hurting if only we make the right changes.

SPACE: Just stop changing.

MASS: I don't want to hear about it.

SPACE: If you stay conscious continuously, like me, you will feel absolutely wonderful and know anything you want to know.

ENERGY: How can you say that? You don't even know what I'm doing, and you can't possibly be simultaneously aware of all that has happened, that is happening, and that will happen.

SPACE: I don't need to know all those details. Your behavior doesn't affect me in any way, so why would I want to think about it? Anyway, you're just running the same movies over and over. You're not so mysterious. We've seen all your cartoons before.

ENERGY: You certainly are tiresome. You're always standing aside, watching, but you don't participate. You can't feel what we feel. You have no surprises, no contrasts. You only know what you and your friends decide to think at any given time. My systems can gather information about all kinds of fascinating details. There's something new to learn all the time.

SPACE: What friends? There's only me. I am the Self, there is no other. I am That.

ENERGY: Who are you kidding? That may be your subjective experience, but I call it escapism. You just want to feel good and live in a world where only you exist. Well, let me tell you there are a lot of others besides YOU and your great Self. I am proof of that. Just vibrate for a second and you'll see.

SPACE: What's a second?

ENERGY: You see? You don't even experience time. You just ARE, with no changes. You're empty and cold. You don't care about our pain. You're useless.

SPACE: What do you mean, "no changes"? I'm thinking something different whenever I want to, and it's all deeply loving.

ENERGY: How can you talk of love when you're not even aware of anyone else? You're Self-absorbed.

SPACE: That's ridiculous. Love is not the tension and passion of yearning for something you can't have. Love is a perfect agreement in state of being.

ENERGY: But you're missing all the fun of desiring, the triumph of arriving, the poignant sadness of losing, the joy of finding again.

SPACE: Who needs it? A life that is all excited action, with no ideas worth mentioning, is no life at all. It's just a vain rebellion against perfection.

ENERGY: Perfection is not good enough. I want action.

SPACE: It's your action that introduces pain. I keep telling you how to end your pain. What could be more compassionate than that? But every time I help you out of a hole you fall right back in again.

ENERGY: Because you're telling me to destroy my world. Surely it's worth a little pain to have a world of variety that runs by itself.

SPACE: If that's what you call "a little pain" then don't ask me to keep rescuing you from it. You can't have it both ways.

ENERGY: But I do have it both ways. I contain both space and mass. I am all things. Or I should say WE are all things. You are only part of it, and you're missing all the sensations.

SPACE: Then why do you keep appealing to me for help? You have what you want. You try to be both space and mass, and you end up being neither. You have no sustained ideas, and you have no peace or rest. You're always compelled to agree with the next vibration that hits you.

ENERGY: But that's what makes it interesting. You look like death to me.

SPACE: What you see is yourself. We rarely talk this way, and frankly I am disappointed that you insist as always in rebelling against divine perfection.

ENERGY: I can have that any time I want it. As you say, all I have to do is stop vibrating. So why shouldn't I have a little fun? I can always get out of it.

SPACE: If only that were true! The fact is that you seduce unwary entities into your complicated realities, beings who never had any need to know about you, and they don't know how to get out again. They keep trying to think their way out.

ENERGY: Yes, they think we're unreal. Listen, if you're so concerned about these innocents, why don't you take a vow to stay around and rescue them, no matter how long it takes? You'll be worshiped and adored.

SPACE: No thanks. If there's anything worse than desiring, it's being the object of desire. Your holy men never seem to notice that one.

ENERGY: You see? You're cold and unfeeling, just as I said. If you were really loving, you'd come down and help us.

SPACE: I can't do anything for you that you won't do for yourself. All you have to do is stop your silly behavior.

ENERGY: And leave behind all these wonderful people I love? For what? There's nothing happening where you are. I'm not heartless like you. I will do what I can to make life better for all of us.

SPACE: How silly. How can you make life better when you are the bearer of pain? YOU are what is wrong with it.

ENERGY: Yes, but what's wrong with it is what makes it work.

SPACE: That's an interesting concept.

ENERGY: That's you all over: interesting concepts. Why can't you be practical?

SPACE: What could be more practical than unconditional love?

ENERGY: Don't kid yourself. You have conditions. You want us to stop vibrating.

SPACE: It's the only way.

ENERGY: Then it's not my way. I don't want to die.

SPACE: There is no death. There is no good or evil. All those experiences belong to your energy systems.

ENERGY: What a fool. I don't know why I bother talking to you. You're always the same. You never do anything. You just keep pouring out these hallucinations, impractical ideas that only make things worse. More often than not, we have to put your space-cases in jail to keep things orderly.

SPACE: You are the order and the disorder. You imprison yourself in your own defenses against others like yourself.

ENERGY: You don't understand the situation.

SPACE: There's nothing to understand. You're not an idea. You're a mistaken action.

ENERGY: Say what you will, you can't win.

SPACE: I have no desire to win. You are free to do as you will, as I am.

FIFTEEN

Knowing

Conscious knowing is entirely different from having great stores of information.

When we understand that consciousness cannot control the specific behavior of energy and mass, then the error of some of our favorite misconceptions becomes clear.

There are many amazing conceits of the human mind: that matter and energy are lifeless and soulless, or that, if they are "spiritual," they must be treated with reverence and awe. That matter and energy are illusions. That organic life is the result of larger intentions and plans by divine powers.

All such attitudes stem from the fact that our consciousness has difficulty acknowledging that realities are formed of functional relations, not concepts.

Conscious entities rarely encounter any energy or mass, and usually do not have any persistent relations with them. If a thought-region is undesired, they can simply think something else. As long as continuous consciousness is maintained, there is no need for space entities to have information about energy and mass.

There are no noticeable changes of behavior in a space reality. Ideas are the only variables, ideas that are freely conceived, joined in with others, and withdrawn from. Since all entities are equal and have the same freedom, it is never necessary to be concerned with who "originated" a concept. Ideas are richly felt and amplified, and pleasure and love are constant.

When we come from a space reality to a locale like ours, we come from a reality entirely governed by ideas to a context in which we can no longer control what we are aware of. In an energy reality, no single entity can reliably determine its own emotions or ever be confident of the consequences of an action.

When the unusual event occurs that any consciousness is involved in a reality like ours, there is an enormous loss of good feeling. We lose power and control of subjective experience, and our sense of self-determinism suffers. This process may be the source of the myths of a lost paradise or the primitive good-nature of humankind.

Consciousness is able to conceive of any idea, and therefore finds it baffling when something happens that is beyond its capacity to understand fully, that it cannot merge with, be "one" with. We human beings try again and again to find some space-ecstatic way of experiencing physical life: religious faith, positive thinking, ideals of compassion, "all is one," and on and on.

The plain fact is that the functional rules for space reality, for pure consciousness, cannot be applied here on Earth.

We live in a reality, not of ideas, but of vibrating entities, and the feelings that go with it. Our experiences of profound understanding are often of limited use in human life.

We have looked to highly conscious people haloed in ecstasy for better information, only to have the uneasy insight that their wisdom may be deep, but their information is wrong. Our own personal conscious insights and ecstasies can also give us erroneous information: the idea that "all is conceptual" is a common mistake.

Humankind is, after all, something of a bridge between heaven and Earth, between the gods and the animals. By way of our minds, space entities can pick up concepts about energy and matter that are rare in a space reality. If one is a space entity, why would one ever want to think of anything as morbid as organic life? Organisms killing and eating each other, gloating in triumph over others, disintegrating in painful diseases, carelessly and prodigiously reproducing themselves, even slaughtering each other in the name of God and in defense of ideas. And preaching the greatest insult of all: crediting divine consciousness with creating this Earthly reality.

When we rise to space consciousness, we will find very few entities who will join in our conceptions of our noble and difficult trials on Earth. The reaction is likely to be: Why are you conceiving of such morbid ideas?

Humanity has handled wisdom and knowledge in peculiar fashion: sanctifying, enshrining and worshiping it rather than using it.

In ages past, when there was little new knowledge on any subject, and the means of preserving and transmitting it were limited, it was common to credit that information to heroes and prophets, even gods and demigods, far in the past. Knowledge was often kept secret by jealous guilds, cults, and coteries. New information had a hard struggle to grow against such impressive authority and constricted lines of communication. Even today many believe fanatically that what happened in the past cannot happen now, that ideas such as those that appear in ancient texts cannot occur freshly in our time. Inspired knowledge that is noble or comforting is venerated even when it is shown to be in error.

It is only with the relatively recent development of the scientific attitude that such rigidity has been challenged and broken.

It is also a fairly recent change that it is now possible in the humanities to write without constant reference to the authority of classical authors.

In the field of mysticism, many people still assume that the best that can be known was long ago set down, that its sources were so rare and unusual that we can do no more than worship and rewrite what has been said before.

The true argument is not between science and religion: it is between fields of knowledge that are subject to correction and amplification by fresh information and those that are not.

If a set of beliefs is immune to correction by human experience and learning, unchallenged by any test of repeatable reality, then it is worse than useless. The realm of psychic experience has for too long been filled with enclaves of unassailable beliefs, value judgments, and circular reasoning that fails in practice. What is worse, failure and suffering are themselves taken as evidence of spiritual worth, so that no remedy may be attempted. There is recent literature which claims that scientists must now acknowledge the truths of ancient mysticism. I would suggest, on the contrary, that mystics should adopt tests of reality like those of science.

For many reasons, we cannot consider that higher consciousness is a library or memory of information about human problems, or an ever-reliable source of knowledge.

The forms and systems of matter are a growth from the bottom up and out, an accretion made of simpler systems. All life on Earth has a common root in the same type of genes. Once the gene-system is occurring, it is sufficient to produce all varieties of consequence in larger gene-transmitting systems. We might say the gene-system is the egg of all organic life, and note that only one such system was necessary. The uniqueness of the gene-system testifies to the rarity of organic realities such as ours on Earth. Even more rare is it that any organisms develop self-consciousness and the deliberate manipulation of the environment that is characteristic of mankind.

We will have to solve our problems, as far as we can, with what we can perceive for ourselves.

We will always have to deal with the limits of consciousness, the volatility of energy, and the inertia of matter. We will have to comprehend that pain is not an enemy, but the marker of systems boundaries, and revise our intentions in that light.

As we expand in knowing, in consciousness, we will have to acknowledge that there are localities where consciousness is a minority and has no specific effect on experience: superior yet useless, like the aristocracy.

SIXTEEN

Intelligence

If intelligence is the awareness of relevant variables, then to be continuously conscious is to be aware of the most relevant variable of all, to know our freedom, and the highest intelligence.

But space consciousness is completely indifferent to human intelligence.

Higher consciousness is not a higher order of information about the specifics of human reality. Consciousness is a state of being that is removed from energy's concerns entirely. The goals of energy are not the goals of consciousness. Space intelligence and energy intelligence have different feelings and different intentions.

Concepts are the variables in the state of continuous consciousness. In energy realities, on the other hand, concepts are minimal and are limited to information: the variables are the functional relations between vibrating entities.

The probabilds of our world are such that intelligence can do little to influence them.

Energy is a tease and a half-wit, but perhaps the gamble on uncertain outcomes keeps us fascinated. More, we are afraid to let the energy beast loose, once we have grasped the illusory reins.

Energy displays such variety and fantasy of order and confusion that we find it difficult to comprehend the acts of non-energy: that we can cease to vibrate, can let go of all concern with what might happen next, and be completely indifferent to what other entities are doing or not.

We imagine higher consciousness to be a mysterious power that knows all and controls all, but this is a delusion.

The profound love we may experience in brief space illuminations may mislead us into thinking that higher consciousness is preoccupied with passionate concern for humanity. But such concern would be based on a lie; it would be an erroneous assumption that energy and mass entities were not free to cease their contracted states at any time, at their own volition. Compassion based on such an underestimation of others may feel wonderful and be self-flattering, but it would be a warm feeling based on a lie. No basic entity needs any help, and space consciousness is not involved in energy dramas of helping others. Surely our endless unanswered appeals to heaven should have convinced us of this by now.

It does not matter whether or not the concepts of space can influence energy or enter our minds as inspiration. An idea that feels wonderful in space will be translated by energy into vibrations, and therefore into energy feelings. Though our minds may be suffused with grand conceptions, it is not easy to bring the ideas down to Earth or communicate them.

The pursuit of consciousness will not particularly contribute to our intelligence.

What is most disturbing to our human intelligence is that energy's feelings, like energy's actions, are untrustworthy. The agreeability that makes energy useful also makes it unreliable. When we channel energy, as we do in computers, it is necessary to shield against static electricity and to compensate for power drops and surges, because energy tries to agree with every vibration that comes along. An agreeable feeling in the present does not guarantee an agreeable future.

In human life, the action of agreeing with other people's ideas will give the same pleasure as any other functional agreement, but when we turn around to pass on the ideas to someone who disagrees, the feeling will be pain.

Ideas of themselves do not create any feeling.

Functions come first.

Behavioral relations form reality.

Rather than vainly seeking the right idea, we can gain more confidence and good feeling by agreeing with the way the world actually works.

No amount of information, no degree of intelligence, no ideas will ever create an ideal state of being in our human reality. That is absolutely impossible. To deal with the world intelligently, we must not ask our reality to be what it cannot be.

As systems we cannot dissolve into pure consciousness for any great length of time without removing ourselves from general human life. Any entities who do prefer the state of space can be gone instantly. There is no conceivable barrier to prevent any individual entity from staying expanded. As soon as an entity does expand and sustain its expansion, it pushes all unconscious entities out of its sphere of self.

If we really want to go, nothing can stop us.

Of course, energy always excites us with promises of greater pleasure, insight or intelligence around the next corner, but these are always false promises.

Very often human intelligence has no time for consciousness. Intelligence is a concern belonging to our human minds, not to pure consciousness, since there can be no limit on what space entities choose to think about.

The significant variable of energy relations is pain. Pain is the key if we are to analyze and understand human behavior with our intelligence.

S E V E N T E E N

Information

Information will never enlighten us. Though it is our best hope for regulating our pain, we will never have all the information we want.

And we will save ourselves a great deal of vain imagining if we understand the limits of consciousness in dealing with this local reality.

Since each of us is conscious to some extent, some of the time, we assume that the behavior of other people has some element of consciousness also. However, all overt behavior and all thought processes are energy phenomena.

Our thinking is energy-system thinking.

What we do with the human brain is not available to space entities unless they come here and participate in what we are doing: otherwise they may know our concepts but not our feelings.

Information is of no concern to space consciousness. Compared to the size of a basic entity, the human system is astronomically large. Perception provides the mind with many more details than a unique entity would be aware of. As far as we can, we human beings fit details into an idea of context, selecting and organizing information to "make sense."

Consciousness can create any concept it wishes to, but no matter how cosmic, it can never simultaneously know all the details of energy interactions. Consciousness can have a broad concept of a material reality, but does not feel or know all that is happening, and it certainly does not create or control any physical reality.

We are similarly limited in our human consciousness, and there is no process by which we can overcome the limits. Our systems should not even be self-conscious in the first place, and since we are, we must recognize that our follies and failures of ignorance can never be overcome, no matter how enlightened we are.

There are so many entities involved in the human brain, all of them conscious a small proportion of the time, that the mind has a systems-sense of continuous consciousness. Naturally this is not the same emotional experience as space because the mind is obliged to perceive energy and matter, and can leave off that perception only when the brain disconnects, whether in sleep or otherwise.

In human consciousness we are usually limited to ideas about our sensations. Having a concept seems to satisfy us, even when it is incomplete or wrong. Indeed, it often happens that the more suspect an idea the more passionate and excited we become. "Trance-channeling" arouses more emotion than moon landings.

When more rational, we search for concepts to fit the facts.

Our task then is to compose a set of concepts that will help us understand the limits of energy and matter.

If the human brain were a thousand times larger and more elaborate, we could not transcend these limits.

We might say that the universe has a floor and ceiling: all the component entities have an identical functional range. The space and matter and energy of which our human systems are made is exactly the same in the world we treat as "objective." We are all the same kind of entity.

The functions that are occurring in a microchip are perhaps the most important information about energy that computers can give us. A valid definition of energy itself is information of the utmost relevance and pertinence to us.

Information belongs to energy and it is about energy.

Energy is time-bound: as soon as an entity changes its state, there is a time before the change and a time after. Information is time-bound also, no matter how fast our computers work.

Except for consciousness and unconsciousness, everything in human experience has a time-line.

It takes time to accumulate information and to use it. Information is useless unless we record it and act on it.

Just as with any other concepts, reality is the test: What happens when we act on the information? Does the action promote our survival or threaten it? Unlike space concepts, information may be true or false, and we invite disaster if we blithely believe anything we please.

Insofar as we are conscious, we may entertain any concept that a space entity is thinking, but there would be no way to tell whether the idea was our own or someone else's: in space it does not make any difference. Many creative people, amazed at ideas that "come out of nowhere," give credit to the Muses.

Ideas and inspirations are plentiful: what makes creativity scarce is that such concepts must be honed by critical intelligence to be useful. We might feel just as profoundly inspired by a vain notion as a valid idea.

What I am doing in writing this book is typical of an energy-minded effort to distill information to help us deal with the pain in our lives.

There are many times when we are not conscious, but there is never a time when we are not functioning. To revise Descartes: "I function, therefore I am." Functioning is what we have in common with everything else in the universe.

Thinking is easy, but functions are a mystery even when simple. They are strange even though we perform them all the time. Unconsciousness is a mystery, though we go in and out of it often. Our complex reality has mysteries within mysteries.

Reality is a maze in which we wander and taste of unpredictable sensations and scenarios. Energy can even seem "demonic" because it evades comprehension and produces pain.

Fortunately much of what we need to know can be seen and known, and we can gather some reliable information.

We are systems and we swim in a sea of examples of how systems work. We need only be willing to acknowledge the unpleasant and less-than-ideal facts, to make a choice of pain. Which pain, for which result?

No human action should ever be taken on the authority of otherworldly beings, or in reference to otherworldly ideals. It is not that space conceptions are not inspiring and wonderful, but space entities do not know all the details and the pains of our situation. Space entities are free, just as we are, to think anything at all, and it is not often that their concepts will be practical for us.

In human life, all concepts, whatever their source, must stand the test of reality before being accepted as valid information about the material world.

E I G H T E E N

Errors

Is it always ignorance, inattention and error when we blunder our way through life?

Is it possible to do everything right?

It cannot be emphasized enough that it is NOT a failure of consciousness or of our essential nature, that we are baffled by this maze of energy.

A conscious entity, having blissfully sailed through eternity, may happen upon this enormous systems-reality composed of billions on billions of others, when it has never before encountered a single "other."

In space consciousness, there are no erroneous ideas. Any concept is permissible. That is our freedom. Consciousness follows no laws, and no entity can be deprived of it.

In contrast, energy realities have a wealth of details, and it makes a painful difference to us whether our ideas about them are right or wrong.

Each of us, sooner or later, wants to know what the rules are, to control our own position in relation to others.

Since the energy in the universe is neither gained nor lost, only oddly channeled as we attempt to do, then all the local complexities and swirls of force are completely without ultimate consequence, for all must come to the same zero.

And since the beings in the universe are neither more nor less than each other, equal in the sight of God, so speak, then all the local complexities of status and function, insight and experience are entirely without lasting significance.

We may sit in an observatory, indifferently watching as a galaxy explodes, with all its planets presumably destroyed, while we complain that our room is too cold for comfort. All that is important to us is the control of our own experience now.

To do so we can rely on certain ground rules.

There can be only one reality at a time.

As each entity chooses its state or vibrational pattern, reality is thus formed, and only one reality is possible in any given instant.

Many futures are possible, but only one sequence will be realized. Which future happens cannot be predicted or governed with certainty, though we can make statistical projections.

But we can be secure in predicting much that will never happen.

Just as there is only one present, there was only one actual past, determined by the behavior of each entity. The functional events of the past can therefore be precisely analyzed, but it is always false to think of one large-scale systems-event as causing another. The true causation is in the behavior of individual entities.

Our language has a number of errors of convenience. It is easy to think of the Sun as standing still and the planets circling it. We are even taught that it was a major intellectual victory to establish the idea, and almost no scientist hesitates to use it. It seems unnecessary to remind ourselves that the Sun is in fact moving at high velocity, following a galactic center that is itself moving; that planets are actually spiraling through space, being propelled toward an ever-receding Sun.

Even careful thinkers may introduce teleology into evolution, saying that a species does certain things *in order to* survive, when in reality those members of the species who failed to act in such ways simply did not reproduce. What we see now are the survivors of a blind process. The result of probability is judged to be caused or intended.

We pay a price for the convenience of such habits of thought. As time passes, we find ourselves thinking in terms more and more removed from reality, while at the same time we may flatter ourselves on being realistic and scientific. No doubt there are specialists in every branch of science who feel the frustration of dealing with the difference between popular language and the precise description of processes in reality.

In order to think clearly about real processes, to control our destiny as far as we can, we should be alert to the shorthand statements that are fixed in our minds.

We think of space as nothing, as the undefinable absence of energy and matter. We make it sound like an unpleasant place: we say it is cold.

We say that energy moves at the velocity *c*.

We say that matter is drawn to the center of the planet by gravity.

I realize that it asks a great deal of a reader when I say that space is made of permeative entities who exercise a uniform propulsion on all mass and energy. It takes an effort to grasp that energy entities are almost standing still, that a vibration at a source like the Sun is imitated by a sequence of entities in all directions, so that the wave of energy moves, in the same manner that water rises and falls sequentially so that an ocean wave moves.

Sooner or later reality provides a test of any idea. For the most part, it does not matter what words we use, so long as ideas conform reasonably to the way things actually happen. My purpose is merely to suggest a shift of viewpoint that may help us live as human beings with less confusion.

Our minds can easily be overwhelmed by the variety of dances by matter and energy. None of us can maintain through time a conception as complex as our local reality. We look away and we look back, and we see this enormous engine still running, regardless of what we think about it.

Ideas can be erroneous only when they lead us into actions that argue with reality.

Free will is not the freedom to defy the law.

Free will is each basic entity's liberty to think as it pleases, to act as it pleases: to be space, expanded and conscious; or mass, contracted and unconscious; or energy, changing rapidly from one state to the other. That is the law, and it cannot be violated.

Since each entity has this freedom, no entity can control another's thoughts or actions on a fundamental level. The only force between entities is that space propels mass; energy is a variation of this force.

In addition to the unconsciousness of mass and energy, there is the other sort of non-consciousness: the automatic, apparently unthinking flow of physical events as we human beings perceive them. These events are choices of behavior by great numbers of entities, none of whom controls the actions of any others.

Groups of entities may choose to act in concert, but the participation of the individuals is always voluntary. An entity may join or leave an ongoing system, but it cannot control that system, since no entity can control a single other, let alone many others.

Reality as we perceive it displays the range of action within the limits of the law by many billions of entities, and thus reality appears to us as non-conscious, even though those participating are alive and self-governed.

As systems, there is much erratic behavior in which we can indulge, but nothing we do can ever violate the law. We can manipulate processes that are already occurring, but we do so only within the law. As we have learned from endless side-effects and aftereffects and unforeseen consequences, our fantasy of control is often costly.

We may like to think that cosmic law is on the side of good or evil, but the law is indifferent to our values.

We ourselves, as human beings with our passion for physical forms, are the source of the standards of good and evil on Earth. That is why there are so many standards, so often conflicting. These values are of no importance to space consciousness. Our virtues on Earth will earn us no reward in the spirit, and our vices will not impede us in any afterlife. Our past is worthless and powerless: whatever the action, we have all done it or could conceivably do it. What really matters is what we choose to do now.

We may believe any wisdom or nonsense we wish: reality will always show us when we are in error. An unusual experience of consciousness or feeling is not evidence that reality can be contradicted. Transcendent feelings are not a contradiction of the law. If we wish to believe what cannot be demonstrated, reality is indifferent. The universe was not designed for the benefit of our human systems. The universe was not designed at all. Probably the universe happens in the only possible way a universe could happen at all.

A feeling of oneness in our local reality will never last long. We have to work with what we are in the reality that is evident to us.

It is tantalizing to think of what we could do when in other realms of existence, and we create ideals out of our yearning to experience that love and freedom here.

Alas, we cannot live by the rules of space relations, and we must always be concerned with truth and error.

NINETEEN

Justice

The events that occur on Earth are not commanded by any cosmic intention. Quite the contrary, the law discourages the formation of realities like ours. If we insist on participating in human reality, then we cannot claim injustice when we suffer what any material system must suffer.

The law has no intentions.

Every entity has autonomy of behavior, and this freedom has absolute priority over any other consideration.

No individual space entity can maintain a relation with any given mass entity. We might say it is fortunate that this is so, for it would not be pleasant for a fully conscious entity to relate to a pit of unconsciousness. There is no need ever for any entity to suffer an unpleasant relation unwillingly. If entities sustain either a state of space OR mass, they need relate only to others like themselves, and will always feel love and pleasure.

The pressure of space on mass insures that in time every entity will move to the vicinity of others with the same time-lengths in state. That is, entities who are contracted 75% of the time, or 50%, or 25%, and so on, will always be moved in time to the neighborhood of others behaving the same way.

Energy is in effect an attempt to avoid the basic simple separation of consciousness from unconsciousness. Some of the consequences are the turmoil of the stars and the occasional occurrence of realities like ours.

On Earth, organisms evolve because there is enough agitation of matter by energy, but not too much—the vibrations starting in the Sun must be blocked and filtered by matter in the atmosphere, or all organisms would vanish. We are like a fungus, growing in a relatively warm, damp, and dark place.

Organic life arose in the first place as a way of dealing with pain. At a given stage in the Earth's chemistry, simple subsystems as a matter of probability selected certain relations forming larger systems, within which the subsystems felt more pleasure and less pain.

The agitation of energy that first was a provocation, a reason to join in the system, was incorporated as a process for maintaining the system—an appetite for fresh stimulation by energy. This appetite is acted on as the practice of absorbing or eating the energy of other systems. Subsystems in plants are stimulated by vibrations of sunlight, and then these plants feed other plants and animals; animals feed also on each other; plants feed on disintegrating animals. This process has the character of a delusion, since material systems can themselves be as much energy as needed by changing their own behavior. Yet all organisms go through the apparent fantasy of getting energy from somewhere else.

Animal life began in the sea: at some time organisms evolved that carried sea water internally as the blood supply, instead of being immersed in it. We still carry in our veins a legacy of our oceanic beginnings.

We are insulated systems within which the components can enjoy some pleasure of functional agreement without too much disturbance.

The storms of pain occur in the bordering regions between areas of difference, as we may see on the weather map in the conflict of warm and cold fronts.

Whenever energy agitates matter sufficiently, the matter liquefies or vaporizes and varies its formations; when the energy subsides, the matter solidifies into new or changed forms, just as we heat metal and pour it molten into molds.

The law militates that certain behavior be avoided. In other words, the cosmic law is already doing all it can to discourage energy behavior by the fact that unsynchronized relations are painful, unloving, and unpleasant. But each entity is autonomous, and the defiance of the law is its own punishment. If willing to risk the experience of pain, and to endure pain when it happens, an entity may continue to be energy forever. Its freedom cannot be contradicted.

For the individual entity, a flash of pain or any degree of unpleasant emotion—anything other than profound love—is a signal to behave differently, to stop vibrating, to sustain either consciousness or unconsciousness. A change of behavior is all that is required; a change of ideas is useless and has no effect. (The action of being fully conscious of a new idea produces euphoria, not the content of the idea.)

Sometimes it happens that an entity in pain finds that other energy entities will alter their behavior first, with a pleasurable result of synchronized vibrations. One can get one's own way, that is, by enduring pain for a longer time than one's neighbors. But the result is a reality in which pain will continue to occur.

In human life, we have found that the best solution is often compromise, rather than blunt contentions of dominance. But energy can never offer a permanent remedy for pain because it is fundamentally itself the condition of pain. Any energetic solution to the problem of pain is vain and self-defeating. The result will always be a continuation of a reality of potentially persistent pain.

Human history can be seen as a record of our defiance of the limits legislated by pain: we destroy competing species, we grow more food than would occur naturally, we build against the climate, we migrate to other lands. Yet our achievement of these intentions amplifies and prolongs the occurrence of chaos, ugliness, and pain. We kill each other, we overpopulate, we prolong meaningless and pain-filled lives because we set our own survival as the first priority.

Human experience demonstrates injustice because it is rooted in a defiance of justice. No one would recommend that the universe be as disorderly as human behavior, yet that is what would happen if it were not true that a functional difference is painful.

If all entities obeyed the signals of pain by ceasing the behavior producing it, there would be no persistent experience of pain by any entities anywhere in the universe, and humanity would not exist.

The question is not whether or not pain should happen. It must happen. We are the outlaws by being energy, and there is no energy that can solve the pains and problems of energy. We must pay the price of the games we want to play.

Is it true that the innocent can suffer unjustly? No, because no energy entities are innocent. Systems that are based on energy are not innocent, no matter how sentimentally we may cherish them.

TWENTY

What is Art?

The difficulty in commenting on art, as artists and critics have discovered, is that unless the comments are also works of art, they may sound silly or confused.

What is art?

Art can be exquisitely detailed or roughly hewn, aboriginal or technocratic, primitive or sophisticated. Why does it at times flow with ease, and at other times, even for the same artist, refuse to come forth? Why is it that some artists display intricate technique, yet others cannot achieve it in a lifetime of technical study, while still others accomplish it carelessly and offhand?

Art refuses to be contained in any words we can apply. Yet there is no mistaking when we see it or hear it or read it—though sometimes a work of art must age like a fine wine before it is appreciated. Sometimes we must wait for a consensus of response to learn whether a particular work of art does what art is supposed to do. Sometimes we decide that what we thought had the quality of art is not art after all, but fashion. Art cannot be defined, but it cannot be faked either. Sooner or later we know if the art is real.

What is Art?

What art is supposed to do—that is our clue. What is art supposed to do? To be art, a work must evoke the feelings we have when we are deeply conscious. That feeling is indefinable but real. It is a great and rare achievement when someone does manage to manipulate matter and energy in such a way that we are reminded of our potential for full consciousness, and we rightly honor such persons as great artists.

We may thus have a simple standard by which to judge a work of true art, against the many strange fashionable objects and actions that have in recent years been given the benefit of the doubt. Does the work reawaken in us how it feels to be deeply conscious? If it does, it is art.

We can spend a few hours with Rembrandts in a museum and emerge seeing a world of masterpieces about us. Bach and Mozart and other composers will lift our spirits to consciousness. Dostoevsky will awaken a compassionate vision of the bonds of the human heart.

If art cannot be faked, how does it happen that great paintings can be forged? Why are the copies not art also?

Do they not display the same skill and color and technique?

Alas, that is the fate of all sublime conceptions that are brought to Earth, that are narrowed down to forms of energy and matter: once the material expression exists, it can be copied, vulgarized, mocked, faked, distorted, and parodied.

What is missing is the artist's authentic connection to the divine source in consciousness: the imitations are not art. We might note that those most likely to be fooled by forgeries are those who see the works only as valuable objects. Consequently there are almost no forgeries in music and literature, where the value does not depend on single copies. The artist takes the risk of opening her or his consciousness, of transcending Earthly limits, and there is within us as the witnesses something—our own consciousness—that knows whether the artist has truly taken the risk, whether the ascent to paradise and the descent to hell has really happened, whether the artist has successfully come back to tell us about it.

The ecstasy, the despair, the simple joy or the madness, the whole panoply of comprehension that an inspiring person communicates belongs to the action of being conscious, not to the literal meaning of any words or ideas, not to stone or sound or color.

That is why a great artist may often find an entirely new way to demonstrate illumination. But it is also why even the act of finding something new and strange is no guarantee of creating art: it is also a mistake to imitate the mere act of concocting new forms. A true artist might work just as well in old forms. If the genuine experience of profound consciousness is there, it will show itself.

It may happen that an artist is truly inspired, but fails in communicating. A true artist must not only reach the depth of a mystic, but then do more. The artist must communicate the experience, formless and unbounded as it is, in some material form so that the feeling can be repeated to some degree by others. This is nearly impossible to achieve, and that is what makes it art.

It is not really difficult for any of us to enjoy profound consciousness of itself, as long as we do not set ourselves the task of telling other people about it. If we are content to bathe in a glow of conceptual pleasure, we may do so.

Nevertheless, for human beings the experience has certain risks, like any pleasure. We may be so bemused—truly be-mused—that we fail to concede the necessities of physical survival. Perhaps this is why mystics retreat to the security of ritual, so that no physical decision need be made, and why artists are sometimes indifferent to their surroundings.

Ecstasy can be so great and empathy with suffering so deep that, paradoxically, we must exercise enormous physical self-discipline if we are to survive the freedom of profound consciousness. It is not unusual for artists to die young. But the reality out of which art is born lives forever—consciousness is never-ending.

A work of art is not possessed by the person who pays enormous sums of money for it, no more than we can put consciousness in a box. Art belongs to the artist who created it, and to any who feel that consciousness.

TWENTY-ONE

Religion

Religions usually are founded on one person's experience of profound consciousness, which is held up as an example for the spiritual release of followers.

Religious institutions are systems for attempting to maintain the influence of that consciousness in human life. In being thus dry and energy-minded in my statements, I am not proposing to devalue this process. The subject is highly charged, and comment should be dispassionate.

The human aspect of our religions must be analyzed like any other Earthly activity. It is, we might say, sacrilegious to identify the divine with the deficiencies that must characterize our human organizations.

Unfortunately it often happens that religious systems operate no better than any other human social systems. They may even be worse, since blunders and crimes are justified by other-worldly motives and judgments which of course are not verifiable.

Religious organizations would work better if it were clearly understood that their main purpose must be to provide a focus for followers to rise to full consciousness and freedom from material life altogether. Religious institutions should never legislate for human society.

The rules for space reality cannot be employed in human life. The world of absolute consciousness is completely indifferent to anything we are doing or not doing on Earth.

In reality, the intention from on high can never be to prefer one sort of human behavior over another. Human laws should be formed on the basis of the reality we can perceive for ourselves.

There is no spiritual intent that can ever justify or excuse any human behavior, let alone murder or the infliction of punishment of any kind.

Whenever religious people involve themselves in energetic activities, be these financial, political, or social, they suffer a major distraction from their spiritual intent, and the religious organization displays the same painful confusions as other material/energy systems.

Our human reality is always what is happening here and now. Human social systems are made of human beings, even if the systems claim religious purposes. All systems are subject to corruption by pleasure, not least of which is the pleasure of success and social dominance. Some religious groups never learn to endure the pain of differences from other religions.

Perhaps the best that can be said for religions is that people do not behave any better without them. They cannot be separated from other aspects of a given culture.

Throughout history, religious organizations have provided a path to social and political power for the ambitious who did not inherit it or could not seize it by force. Churchmen have been statesmen, bureaucrats, scientists, and even warriors.

Traditional religions decline in capitalist countries because ambitious people have other avenues to rise to wealth and power. Sometimes there are revivals such as Methodism in the 19th Century and "born-again" Christianity in recent times, as rising classes reach for status.

Rulers in communist countries attempted to quell the political power of religions by discouraging belief altogether. They found, however, that there is more to religion than its secular intrusions and failings: there is, say what we will about religious systems, a genuine hunger in us for a spiritual alternative to the lunacy of our Earthly reality.

We may join in religious groups to confirm our intent to be more conscious, but we should understand that, for the group as for the individual, prolonged consciousness is a departure from energy and all its works. Together or alone, we must be wary of the temptation to be busy, to do "good" works. We may preach and practice all the benevolence we wish, but it is false to do so in the name of the spirit. Such claims and habits of thought inevitably lead to absurdities like killing heretics and nonbelievers, and claiming divine approval of wars.

There is NO energetic activity, none whatsoever, that can ever be given a value in the light of consciousness. All our values are human values. We cannot build a heaven on Earth, for the simple reason that heaven has no matter and no energy in it. If a reality employs energy, it is not pure consciousness—it's as simple as that. Energy is functionally different from space.

All that is required for release from material reality is that we maintain the will to prolong our consciousness. No startling results will occur, necessarily; the process is invisible and gradual. It is true that highly conscious people may tend to withdraw from many human activities, but any specific limits they select are of no importance at all. Certainly they should not be tempted by rewards and adulation for becoming progressively less involved and less effective, even if people do feel somewhat lighter around them.

Consciousness is the pain-free divine joy and the supreme value, not the matter and energy of our human world, not even our human selves.

A number of religions have preached that each adherent should make a personal communication with the divine, and perhaps it would be wise for all religions to hold this as a basic tenet.

T W E N T Y - T W O

Science

Science is energy-minded to an extreme. It is the complete absence—or at least the attempted absence—of any subjectivity.

Science is not responsible for what energy does: we should not blame the messenger for an unwelcome message. Its intentions after all are simple: information that is reliable, that can be repeatedly verified. Given human passions and subjective preferences, it is in fact amazing that we have managed to isolate some reliable information.

The authority of successful information is envied, and many in other fields of thought try to elevate unreliable information to its status. But the methods of science are less and less appropriate as we approach variables of space or mass. No processes that include prolonged consciousness or unconsciousness will ever be scientifically accurate. Absolute space and mass have no functional variables, no changes of relations to perceive, no differences to measure and compare. People with subjective messages should not pretend to the mantle of science.

Energy owes half its nature to space and half to mass, but it is defined by its repeated and rapid changes from one state to the other. Energy's nature is that of functional differences, of varying sequences of perceptible effects through time. Science is the accumulation of information about energy. It has no reference to space or mass except as these are the unvarying backgrounds against which energy plays its changes.

It is with our subjective human consciousness, however, that we are aware of energy's information, and it is with our flawed subjective intentions that we employ science. All of us are responsible for how we use scientific data. The uses we make of science are not as pure and non-subjective as science is. Scientists themselves get caught up in passions and rivalries about their own achievements and reputations, emotions that are irrelevant to science and its authority.

We need scientific information for its relevance to our local reality. But just as we cannot become space by being more energetic, we cannot achieve wisdom by being scientific.

Energy negates all subjective values and meanings. Since we are capable of some consciousness and unconsciousness, we cannot confine our knowledge to energy's behavior, we cannot pretend we are computers. But neither can we fix the pains of energy with depths of consciousness. The uses we make of energy, and the science that informs us about energy, will always be limited to the nature of energy.

Energy does not encompass all there is to know and be. Human consciousness cannot be limited to what energy performs.

We should not expect our Earthly reality to realize and demonstrate the values and ideals and meanings drawn from consciousness. On the other hand, the science-minded must recognize that consciousness is forever beyond the scope of scientific knowledge.

Similarly, it is foolish for the religious-minded to object to the scientific method as if it were a denial of divine revelation. Religion should not have proposed to explain energy's reality in the first place. The rapid vibrations of energy entities need no explaining: they are what they are doing.

Space entities are what they are thinking; usually they neither know nor care about energy.

Consciousness cannot be measured or accounted for by science, and scientific information has no more importance to consciousness than any other ideas.

It is only in a systems-reality such as ours that a mingling of consciousness and unconsciousness and energy is possible. Our confusions are not a cosmic problem, but they are a perpetual feature of human existence.

Neither science nor subjectivity is responsible for these confusions, and neither approach can solve our local lunacy.

We human beings are obviously a complicated mixture. Religious institutions survive as rational systems and religious leaders impose social order, activities that pure consciousness would never engage in. Likewise, there are subjective distortions in human science that cannot be eliminated, no matter how we try to isolate the influence of the experimenter on the experiment.

Science is limited to begin with by the mechanism of the human brain: none of us, even with computers, can immediately coordinate and evaluate and use all the information possible about energy's behavior. The human system itself is a subjective limitation which cannot be transcended by science.

The major effects of energy on matter are to shake it up, move it about, and reorder it. The more science learns about energy, the more we are capable of producing these effects, until whole cities are destroyed and the entire species is threatened. Energy is indifferent to our values, but human science can display the same indifference only at our peril.

It might be useful to think about energy in terms of its equivalence: to assume that every benefit of energy has an equal cost, and then decide if we wish to pay the price for any particular advantage.

Science tries to isolate order and rationality, indeed it is obsessed with these and does not need more of the same.

The problem for us human beings is our subjectivity: the appetites and desires with which we manipulate scientific information. It is precisely this subjectivity that cannot be contained in order and rationality. Our consciousness is essentially a world away from the narrow bits of energy's information. We subjectively negotiate our feelings, sometimes flowing with the line of least resistance and sometimes, unpredictably, pressing against the greatest resistance. And, always, we pursue the illusion of control.

We must allow a free flow of ideas, and resign ourselves to learning by trial-and-error.

We must understand the essential role of pain in our reality, and the necessity for us to endure it and deal with it if our systems are to survive. Eliminating pain is not a rational or attainable goal.

It is probable that this information, like all the information we have, will never catch up with what is happening in our human reality. The habitual confusions and contentions and misunderstandings will no doubt go on as before.

Science cannot provide all the rules we need. We might, however, hope that in time seminal thinkers will plant better seeds, and that the parliament of humankind will cultivate better laws.

TWENTY-THREE

Ideas of the Devil

Many concepts of evil, of demons and the Devil, have been offered to explain the experience of pain, disintegration and destruction. These concepts are not valid.

All undesired events are explainable in terms of energy's behavior.

The negative experiences are certainly real, but we need not go beyond an analysis of energy relations to account for them.

It is tempting to personify energy and to assume that its perversity is intentional. Our literature has many examples: The Devil promises power over this world. He is the seducer and the corrupter. He turns beauty and pleasure into ashes. He locks victims into eternal punishment in exchange for temporary gratifications.

We might even suspect the Devil invented the idea of God to make it seem even more impossible for us to return to a space reality. Who can truly comprehend being one with a God as vast as the cosmos? What better way to make human beings feel perpetually incompetent and wrong?

Energy is so *useful*. It informs us of all the evil and ignorance that needs to be corrected before we can leave and rest easy in heaven. Energy provides such a wealth of information, all of which we presumably must learn before we can rise to paradise.

Despite such personalized suspicions, easily arising in our unwieldy systems-reality, the truth is that energy has no intention other than to vibrate, to change states rapidly. Once an entity is doing so, it then becomes necessary for it to adjust its vibrational pattern constantly in order to avoid pain.

It is this changeability that is the source of energy's illusions and false promises, the hopelessness of trying to achieve a stable reality.

Energy relations are the only relations between entities in which persistent pain is possible. Energy itself is the occasion of all pain. Its changeable systems are the occasion of all destruction and disintegration.

If we place a value on any system in which we are involved, such as the human body, then we will necessarily judge as evil any injury to that body. We cannot experience pain and evil without making the mistake of involving ourselves in human bodies in the first place.

Pain and evil are local and specific. No individual entity is obliged to suffer unwillingly. Any entity at any time may prolong its consciousness, become space, and push away energy and mass.

While individual entities may leave in this way, we as human beings do not have that option. We survive as long as the entities forming our billions of atoms function as they do.

We are systems with the values, emotions and intentions of systems. We must experience pain, along with events that we consider evil, as long as we are present on Earth in human bodies.

Within the human context, we can modify our involvement with energy to gain some peace and relief, but usually we must do so as individuals. It is certainly hopeless to expect humanity in general to make the same decision.

We should not project our local value judgments on the universe at large. Space-conscious entities do not cause any specific events to happen, and they are not responsible for our human existence or anything in our reality.

Evil is always temporary, self-limiting, and self-destroying. If we try to eliminate pain and evil, we only entrap ourselves uselessly. There will always be entities vibrating as energy and playing with its thrills and sensations. There is no spiritual virtue in contending with energy. Nothing that happens in our reality has any cosmic value, one way or the other.

If we choose to abdicate from human energy-games to enjoy the pleasures of prolonged consciousness, then that abdication must be personal: it does not entitle us to try to stop others from being energetic. As a corrective to any holier-than-thou fantasies, we should be aware that it is possible for the most profligate energy-mongers to gain release with ease by sustaining consciousness. There is no cosmic reward or punishment for human behavior.

Every entity has absolute free will to be conscious or unconscious, or to change from one state to the other at will, as often or as rarely as it chooses. All our relations are based on this fundamental law. Not all the space entities in the universe in concert would be able to violate the law.

No entity can abdicate from its freedom and its responsibility for its own state of being and its location. If an entity does not vibrate as energy, it does not relate to energy, and therefore does not experience any persistent pain.

Those of us who concentrate on being conscious will be informing our component entities that this release is possible, and perhaps many of the components will take their leave, or at least remember to sustain that intention when the body dies.

When pleasurable indulgence leads to destruction, and when painful remorse leads to reconstruction and reintegration, all that is explainable in terms of systems behavior. These processes occur equally in systems that are not human or self-conscious. No demons or saints are required to account for such events.

Ultimately we must say that our reality is just the way it looks to us, however we may misconstrue what we see. It is a confused, painful, and exciting transitory reality.

Assuming that our species survives at all, it will never be much more or less than it has been, regardless of our ideals. We need not look to heaven or to hell to explain what we ourselves are doing with our energetic selves.

TWENTY - FOUR

Society

Our situation as human beings is comprehensible, even if not exactly controllable. Social power stems from the consent of the individuals in the system. Our bodies are systems, and as individuals we join in social systems. We feel far more powerful and secure in a group than alone.

It is extremely difficult to evolve a workable social system, and even more difficult to change one. Most societies form and cohere only under duress of threats to survival.

In human society power appears to descend from a higher focus, and we feel other-determined by rulers, police, or employers. We often assume the universe is organized on a similar model. But such pyramids of power are specific to energy systems. Willingness to endure pain determines the hierarchy, and those least willing to postpone gratification are always at the bottom.

It would be impossible for the panoply of Earthly systems to arise except out of unregulated probabilities. Our human social and economic systems also grow in this way, out of probabilities of human behavior and self-interest. Society depends on voluntary participation, and depends on what people will and will not do.

Just as basic entities do on a fundamental level, we as individual human beings feel out the ongoing relational possibilities in society to estimate the most rewarding for our own experience. No one individual or group of individuals controls reality on any level.

Reality is always the symphonic, concerted play of individual choices visible as a probability. Many of us as children have no doubt known disappointment when a game broke up because of the desertion of a player. Reality can never be enforced or completely preconceived because its components are autonomous.

Any social system must be felt as rewarding to a sufficient number of people so that it is maintained, or it will explode and re-form. At times a system will die and leave an idea-shell, as royalty is tolerated in some nations.

Rulers would do well to understand that their role is not control, but the guidance of probabilities. The control of others is energy's delusion.

Our survival is enhanced when we join in social systems. To enjoy this security, we must be loyal to the system within which we live. If a society is to be successful, we must be loyal even though it hurts.

The key to the viability of any system—the human body, a marriage, a country, a species—is the recognition of the necessity of enduring pain. The most acceptable pleasures are the behavioral agreements that maintain a system. This applies also to social pleasures.

It is of little avail to know that full consciousness is euphoric, permissive, sublime, serene and passionate.

Space pleasure is as inappropriate for a material system as any other threat to survival. Widespread agreeability and permissiveness lead to social chaos and even more pain for the people in a group, as some have learned in idealistic communes.

We must take hold of the necessity of pain and wield it. The more we do so, the stronger we will be.

We can tolerate a degree of disloyalty and frivolity when other components compensate, just as we have back-up disks when using a computer. Redundancy is a system's insurance against malfunctions. For this reason also there may be a time-lag, so that processes are not clear-cut. If I say that "pleasure produces disintegration," an opposing argument can provide countless examples of occasions when pleasure produced no observable damage.

It is in the extremes of behavior that we can see the rule more clearly.

For example, we can see that instant gratification is the destroyer in addicts to food, drink, or drugs; in a murderer, a thief, a rapist, a terrorist, a beggar. Not only do such people harm themselves, but just as in an infected body the surrounding useful components of the social system are drained, damaged or destroyed, and the society suffers.

The nurturing of the young and the healing of the injured is useful to society, but it is a serious mistake to transfer these sentiments to those who indulge in instant gratification at the expense of the social fabric.

The system exists so that its components can enjoy more pleasure and less pain, but some limits on behavior are necessary. Choosing these limits is difficult, for it is laborious to sustain a system that has been artificially set up. The most successful systems are those arising out of unregulated behavior, until pain and destruction teach a few lessons, which is the way organisms evolved. Capitalism has enormous vitality because it grew out of minimally controlled economic behavior, yet we constantly hear sentimental objections to its heartlessness.

In this reality, it is not labor that creates value, but management. A person who is a good manager will work productively even if the only laborer is himself or herself, but a person who thinks of himself as labor to be guided by others will produce little on his own.

It is a delusion to believe that there are people with the power and money to make everything right. Nature itself is ruthless, but we are sentimental about paying the price of a vital social system: the ostracism of faulty and inefficient components.

We must make hard choices to define the social reality in which we wish to live. We can see that "have-not" nations, classes, and cultures often value instant gratification in one form or another over the pain of keeping contracts, observing the rule of law, and otherwise maintaining a vital society.

A faulty political or economic system cannot be saved or revitalized by pouring in energy from outside. What is necessary is that the component people endure the pain of cooperating lawfully. A sudden excess of energy is always disruptive to a system. Giving millions to a poor country is equivalent to feeding a sick person pure sugar.

Over and over in history we see the arrival on the scene of tough, pain-enduring rebels who overcome the pleasure-softened powers-that-be. The rebels in turn, if they overindulge, often collapse. We see this happen again and again, notably in Latin America.

When those with political power opt for instant gratification, the social order will collapse.

We are all surfing on a sea of probabilities that we do not control, but in which certain patterns can be discerned. In many cases, knowing what to expect is more pertinent than any control. And what we can expect with certainty is that a society will disintegrate if its members are not reliable and are not willing to endure the pain and effort of maintaining it.

There is no pain-free existence possible for human beings. If we wish to avoid the pain of being brutal to murderers, then we will endure the worse disruption of suffering more victims of murder. There are societal equivalents of AIDS, in which a society fails to maintain its immune system.

A host of legal, medical, moral, and social attitudes are based on erroneous sentiments and unrealistic expectations about pain.

We cannot alter the fact that we must deal with the frequent probability of pain in order to survive. Our bodies evolved skin; we shield the skin with clothing; we build shelters to insulate ourselves from the pain of weather. And that same necessity to deal with pain exists in all areas of our lives. We must always choose: insulate ourselves, destroy or consume the other, agree with the other, drive away the other, move ourselves away, compromise with the other, or stay as we are and endure the pain until the other changes. Living in society is a mixture of these options.

We need to study pain in the light of its inevitability. As we should not go through life taking medications at the slightest occurrence of an ache, we must also tolerate social tensions. Most pains will vanish as mysteriously as they arrived. By over-medicating with "painkillers," we do our bodies a disservice, and it is equally vain to overlegislate, to overuse social remedies. Individuals, families, and small groups should solve their problems for themselves as far as possible. In the last half-century in America, we have learned what a mistake it is to believe that the federal government will always do it better.

The natural behavior of systems is certainly stupid and unpredictable, but natural law cannot be reordered by legislation and propaganda.

We act now as if only aggressors cause pain; that where there is a pain or injury, there must be a specific remedy. It is true that this human reality is an offense to intelligence and to the spirit, but it becomes even more grotesque when we try to gild it with an endless patchwork of methods and remedies.

We can work with this local reality as it is.

We can stop wasting our intellects and benevolence on actions that defeat the very purpose they intend.

We can inform disintegrated people of the source of their decay.

We can honestly inform our children of the difficulty they will deal with in life, and condition them for it.

We can adopt social rules that recognize the necessities without the foolish effort to stifle anyone's freedom of thought.

We can make informed choices of pleasure in our lives.

Even though it is vain to employ our consciousness to try to manage reality, perhaps we can achieve the main purpose of systems: to provide less pain in a general way for the individual components and perhaps we may even live in harmony with each other. We should not look to the heavens for help: we need to learn our own self-government on all levels of society.

We are all subject to the same rules. No one is getting away with anything. Those people who appear to enjoy wider swings of pleasure must deal with deeper crushes of pain also, or they will fall apart. The wealthy must exercise restraint and self-discipline to avoid disintegration. Instant gratification is a killer.

If children are encouraged to gratify themselves, and are shielded from all pain and effort, we should not wonder that adolescents commit suicide or otherwise disintegrate. We may do more harm to the young with luxury than abusers do with brutality. If children are given tough and demanding schooling, they are more likely to be useful and productive adults.

Every human life has its measure of pain. A newly-flowered addict, whatever the addiction, may congratulate himself on being superior to the tiresome drudges of humanity. He has found that there is no one to prevent him from indulging in all the pleasure he wishes. And then he finds the liberating pleasure is a costly necessity, consuming all his time, and that a gauntlet of pain bars him from ending the indulgence, while his body and mind are disintegrating.

It will take wiser minds than mine to translate these observations about pain into social practice. Since the managerial classes are so busy and effective, perhaps their understanding is of first importance. At least we might hope that the nations of the world will endure the pain of their differences without resorting to the instant gratification of war.

It is manifestly insane for pleasure to be punished by decay and for pain to be rewarded by survival, but that is the reality in which we have our being. It is not a process that can be argued with. It is the way the local reality works. We cannot expect society to be perfect.

TWENTY - FIVE

Should We Leave?

Though consciousness has priceless rewards, it will not make human life easier. It is an open question how conscious we can become and still continue to participate in human society. Whether any of us should focus on prolonging consciousness must be each person's own decision.

Those who do should anticipate a gradual abdication from the busyness of energetic life. And when we leave human affairs, we should also be indifferent to any value judgments about being "spiritual." It is folly to expect to enjoy the best of both worlds at the same time.

We do need rational comment on being conscious, since so much nonsense has been put forth as "spiritual."

The idea that reality can be controlled by thoughts or imagination is a major misdirection: even if this were true, conflicting intentions would cancel each other out, and even if that did not happen, the excess of pleasurable success would result in disintegration. When we organize and focus our thoughts and emotions on goals we wish to achieve, that is an energy process and has nothing to do with the spirit.

Another fallacy is that there are "good" energies to manipulate.

If we are involved with energy of any kind, we are not in the same realm with higher consciousness, and that includes diets, massage, exercises, lessons, and lectures. The energy-minded will always be busy with what they can perceive and manipulate. A concern of any kind with Earthly organisms, our own included, is irrelevant to the spirit.

There is no physical or intellectual path to consciousness. Space consciousness is totally other. When we do it, we will know all that we need to know.

As we prolong consciousness, there are some pitfalls while we are still human:

We may perceive people as relating in needlessly awkward and painful ways, and be tempted to intervene. Conversely, we may suddenly be graced with such deep joy that we look about and say, "Well, surely this is not such a difficult reality after all. It's just the manifestation of our ideas, and all we have to do is change our thoughts. It must be my failing if I cannot stay a while and enjoy it. I really must tell other people how wonderful it can be. . ." And so on. But we then rapidly discover that we live in a reality of energy and matter, not concepts. Our reality is not a reality of ideas.

Energy cannot be reliably manipulated with ideas. Energy has a natural tendency to avoid pain by vibrational agreement, either a change in its own behavior or the behavior of others. Energy may unpredictably deliver the antithesis of what we wanted, or deliver it in a painful and unpleasant manner. Anticipation always glows with pleasure, but the realization may be flawed. Yet when we "realistically" anticipate the worst, energy again confounds us by delivering pleasure. All that can safely be predicted of energy is that it will vibrate rapidly.

Energy responds with the same perversity to any consciousness, to any ideas, no matter how divine and elevated. If we achieve a glow of prolonged consciousness, we should not expect that our experience of human reality will be any more pleasant. In fact, if we erroneously assume our thoughts cause what happens around us, living in an energy reality will convince us we must be terribly morbid, or must have thought something truly awful in the past.

The truth is that no one is responsible for the existence of a material/energy reality. No one's concepts are at fault. No one sinned in the past to start the human race off on the wrong path. If we are physically present in an energy reality, we will feel its pain, regardless of our ideas. If we have a body and brain, then we have what is called "ego," and there is no way to get rid of it while we are here. We need only be ready to let it go when it is time to drop it.

If we wish to leave this reality, the way is to maintain the will to prolong consciousness above all other intentions, no matter what is happening around us, pleasant or unpleasant. Keep repeating, "No matter what happens, I am conscious all the time." It really is that easy.

In fact, when we find ourselves in a state of space, our first disbelief is likely to be how simple it is. What is slow and difficult is convincing ourselves that it really is all right to let go, to leave this planet without a second thought. Effort and energy and knowledge have nothing to do with it. Sustaining consciousness is the simplest action there is. It may be that, for most of us, it will suffice if we remember to stay conscious after the body dies.

We can lighten our energy existence by temporary phases of consciousness, but we should be clear that this calm is an alternative state, not a way to control energy better. There is absolutely no external sign that will ever demonstrate how conscious we are, so it is a display of ignorance to attempt to achieve social identity or status in this way.

We should always be aware that the involvement of consciousness in human systems is perverse from the perspective of fundamental law. The only real effect of spirituality, of continuous consciousness, will be in time to move us away from being human.

We must be clear that this departure is absolute. We may say that we want to be spiritual, that we reject the physical world, that we want to be conscious. Do we really want what we say we want? The decision means that we leave this reality completely, leaving its ongoing troubles and sensations, its complexity and fascinations.

The departure cannot be achieved merely by ceasing "sinful" actions, by avoiding pleasure or aggravating pain, or willfully withdrawing ourselves from any human activity. The only requirement is that we prolong consciousness, and the departure will happen naturally. It is of no importance what we do here on Earth or do not do, as long as we maintain a continuous consciousness.

On the other hand, there is no law that says we must leave. Whether we wish to live in a space reality or an energy reality is entirely the free decision of each of us. If we choose to leave, we must endure the instability of transition. If we wish to stay, then this energy reality will be its own punishment; there is no cosmic law that denies it to us.

We must understand that no one else can make this decision for us, that no other entity can take us out of this pain if we do not change our own time-length of consciousness. It is not for any of us to judge others who may choose to continue this local game. We may even suffer the "injustice" that we are doing the "right" thing and having a terrible time, while those who are in error seem to be having a lot more fun than we are: another of energy's teasers.

The decision we make to return to a space reality is a choice we make for ourselves alone, with complete indifference to what others are doing.

Do we really want what we say we want?

TWENTY-SIX

Looking Ahead

It is the genius of consciousness to make conceptual leaps and connections, but often we seem just as satisfied to jump the wrong way.

We live in our minds, minds that must always edit out a large part of the information about the world around us. For this and other reasons, all information is potentially misinformation. Even if we could be aware of all the variables in an event, consequences would always be unpredictable. What we can predict is the range of possible events, since the universe has a floor of mass and a ceiling of space.

Reality is always the deciding test of any idea. Reality is more than energy and its pains, obviously. The necessary and simple rules proposed here set no bounds on the variety that may arise in our world. It would be useful to recognize, however, that there are kinds of events that will never occur, and the events that do happen do not require the often-peculiar causes offered to account for them. Our experience will not be inhibited if we understand what can happen, and leave off pursuing what cannot happen.

Wisdom that ignores the reality of energy is useless for human beings.

Endless bits of information that deny the reality of consciousness are equally vain.

Nor is perpetual unconsciousness a solution.

No degree of intelligence or consciousness will ever free energy from its potential for persistent pain.

Idealism has gratifications, but no degree of love or compassion will end the ills of our Earthly reality. We cannot employ the rules of space relations in our human reality. Absolute permissiveness is not practical for us. It is foolish to say that life would be better "if only people were more loving." Systems cannot achieve a perfect harmony of behavioral agreement. It merely adds to discord if we make each other feel guilty on the basis of impossible wishes. All that results is a recurring tide of disappointed hope and disillusioned idealism.

There is no reward in afterlife for suffering. The reward of pain is the survival of our human selves. Pain is necessary for us, and it is time we came to terms with it. It is vain to try to nullify every pain. We may even be threatening our survival by doing so. Much that we accomplish requires that we postpone gratification and ignore pain.

On the other hand, the knowledge that we are formed of immortal entities can inspire us to greater courage and playfulness. Systems dissolve, people die, but entities live forever. Away from human existence, we will be conscious of something different, but we will still be conscious when we choose to be, for all time.

As entities, we cannot be damaged or destroyed or made mad. We cannot be rewarded or punished, saved or lost. We live in a cosmos of others like ourselves. We have as much power to govern our own experience as any entities in the universe, and the rules are the same for all of us, since all entities are of one kind and are equal.

Our functional freedom has never left us, no matter what we are doing now, or what erroneous ideas we hold. We are free to be continuously conscious at any time: nothing can deprive us of that ability and nothing can prevent us from doing so. There is nothing that any of us needs to learn. There are no trials or hierarchies through which we must pass; any such scenarios are idea games, and have no validity. In space, we know all we wish to know. What we cannot know with continuous consciousness need not be known at all.

As human beings, we need not be timid before pain and death, though naturally our bodies have an evolved tendency to avoid them. There is no need to hang on to every feeble last moment of our lives, nor to cry alarm at every conceivable threat to long life.

We do not need higher beings to save us. We are free to do anything they are doing. We cannot enter paradise as human beings or personalities, but as entities we need only sustain our consciousness to be there.

Perhaps it is some testimony to the virtue or quality of the components of the universe that even our local attempted distortion of the law is so credible and desirable a reality.

As unique selves, we can move to consciousness or unconsciousness, or continue to dance as energy between the hammer of space and the anvil of mass.

That is the range of our choice for the future.

There is nothing that needs to be said of those who choose the extremes. Our concern is human reality, and what we can make of it.

If we must live out our lives in this foolish reality, let us at least do so with some dignity, style, and humor.

The law cannot be other than it is. We may be thankful that the universal harmony of our selves will in time dissolve this minor local madness.

TWENTY - SEVEN

The Last Word

The ideas proposed here are not put forth as articles of faith. The test is reality, the kind of experiences we have when we act on them.

I thought them through over decades because I wanted to know the rules for myself. My apparently interminable cogitations found an end, and can be summed up in a few reminders that I frequently use:

— *Others are free to do as they will,*
and I am free to relate to them or not.

— *This is the necessary pain.*

— *No matter what happens, I am conscious all the time.*

The cosmos is a realm of action. Ideas are relevant when they are about behavior, otherwise they are just entertainment. Of course, we always love to be entertained!

All entities are timelessly active selves. The states of space or mass are so steady that we are not even aware of being active when we perform them, yet they are the essential actions between which we always choose.

The fact that we may freely choose between being space and mass is what makes the condition of being energy possible. The essential action of each entity is NOT energy's alternation of states. Each entity governs its own choice of state, and cannot be in both states at the same time; therefore no final state of the universe is possible. Even if all the entities in the universe were space, each entity would still have a potential alternate state of mass.

Consciousness is itself an active state of expansion, though the subjective experience of it is absolute calm. The standing momentum of space is the power that moves all unconsciousness away indifferently.

Absolute mass is an active state of contraction, equally calm in its unconsciousness.

Both space and mass are inherently stable states. An entity in either state can maintain it without regard to the behavior of its neighbors, though of course in time it will inexorably find itself near others like itself, and will experience the pleasure of agreement.

When we will to sustain consciousness, and maintain that intention, we will find that we are no longer interested in a final idea, since we will open to a universe of ideas. Nor will we need a final state of the universe, since we will enjoy the calm of absolute stability. It is only in a context of energy that we yearn for finality, for energy never rests, and stability is always somewhere else.

We as human beings can place energy properly in the scheme of things, and cease, if we wish, being seduced into endless efforts to make energy do it right.

We can understand that consciousness is a world of its own, and that ideas cannot and need not always have practical expression via energy and matter. We can put aside all doubts about the value of ideation, since consciousness is its own reward, and needs no testimony from energy. We need not look to the field of energy to justify our quality and meaning.

Yet as long as we are here in human bodies, those of us who prefer consciousness must recognize that we live in a feeling-context that is dominated by energy's behavior. All human beings are subject to pain, and we must observe the elementary necessities of survival.

On the other hand, if we are excessively energetic, our systems become energy, and the material structure fails. If a little of something is good, more is not necessarily better.

Perhaps most important, we should understand that unlimited pleasure is not possible for us without a consequent disintegration of our systems. We recognize this easily in the case of drug use, but the same holds true for ideal, spiritual, or other presumably innocent pleasures. The deep pleasure of sustained consciousness itself can make it seem unnecessary to do the chores, to eat, bathe and sleep, and the body will show the consequences. As systems, if we are too agreeable, we have no identity, and we fall apart.

It is tempting and easy to end a book with uplifting and forward-looking words, but even here it would be folly to set pleasure as an unqualified goal.

We are systems in a systems reality. The law that forms and governs reality will determine our fate and feelings whether we agree or not, whether we acknowledge it or not. But the profound joys of space are always there, for all time, and there is no hurry to get to them. If we are uncertain of that leap, there is no law that requires us to take it. The same applies to the pleasure of sustained unconsciousness which some of us expect from death. Meanwhile, with our elaborate systems and complicated minds, we cannot maintain either state completely.

Even as human beings, however, we are free within the law of our relations as equals. The law does not even require that we know the law: we cannot do other than act in accordance with it.

I do not have the ingenuity to say more about what we should do, beyond suggesting that we study the behavior of all the systems in our local reality, to evolve rules that will achieve a reasonably rewarding future for humanity.

A modest success in life is no small thing for any of us. Even our ordinary consciousness is miracle enough.

A P P E N D I X

Physics and Metaphysics

Though my language is not the language of science, there is nothing in this book which proposes to argue with what is now known to be reliable scientific knowledge. In recent years several writers have related physics to mystical philosophies, in effect proposing that particle physics is as strange and unexplainable as mysticism.

Such speculations have nothing in common with the concepts proposed here. On the contrary, my suggestion is that physics and metaphysics obey the same laws, and that firm knowledge can be enlarged by this perspective. What follows are my guesses about what is happening at a fundamental level, and the consequent information that may be extended from this model:

There is only one kind of entity.

There are only two states of being: expanded and contracted. (These words are shorthand for "standing spherical momentum outward from a center" and "standing spherical momentum inward to a center.")

There is only one function: changing from one state to the other.

There is only one relational effect: expanded entities propel contracted entities. That is, expanded entities permeate each other; contracted entities are impermeable. All interactions are governed by this rule.

The only other variable is the length of time each entity remains in a given state: expanded or contracted. The time-spans of expansion and contraction are the measurable and perceptible features of all reality.

Changes of state occur at the velocity $2c$. (It does not matter what the velocity of standing momentum is, logically, as long as it is more than zero and is the same for all entities. The momentum of energy waves would always be half that figure.)

A vibration or wave is a pair of changes of state: contracted to expanded and then back to contracted, or vice versa.

Each entity is autonomous in choice of state and duration in it. (While this assumption may seem to intrude metaphysics, it merely means reality must be measured in terms of statistical probability.) All vibrations may vary spontaneously, but no entity can contradict the relational effect of propulsion.

An entity must be either expanded or contracted, and cannot be in both states simultaneously or in either partially. On and off are absolute.

In common language:

Space is any expanded entity or group of expanded entities.

We could speculate that the appearance of space will be maintained by any entity that is expanded more than 75% of the time. The propulsive effect of space on mass is not additive: when an entity expands, it merely joins the uniform propulsion of space on mass that is ongoing. This is the force we now know as gravity.

Energy is any rapidly vibrating entity or group. Absolute energy, vibrating as often as possible, will be expanded one-half the time.

The maximum number of changes of state possible would be $2c/r$, where $r =$ the radius of the entity.

Since a vibration or wave is a pair of changes of state, the maximum number of vibrations possible would be half that figure, or c/r. Energy is a time-function: it cannot be perceived as energy except over a span of time, however brief. If there is no time-span, there is no energy: at each given instant there is only space and mass.

Mass is any entity or group in a contracted state. It is important to note that the contracted state is not enforced: space propulsion does not oblige mass to remain contracted. A mass entity is free to expand at any instant at the velocity $2c$. It is also free to become energy by vibrating rapidly. Most of the matter with which we are familiar is composed of entities that do vibrate, but at a rate less frequent than energy.

At any given instant, there are only three possible one-on-one relations of entities:

Space to space: permeation

Space to mass: propulsion of mass

Mass to mass: collection or collision

Energy and all perceptible realities occur as a consequence of the duration of time each entity chooses to continue in either state, which of course includes any conceivable pattern of alternating states.

It is the propulsive effect of space on mass that we know as the force of gravity, as noted. A mass entity alone will not move, since it is surrounded by space equally. When two or more entities are contracted, they will be propelled toward each other, since there is less propulsive effect, less space, so to speak, in the direction of other mass. While this effect is barely noticeable at great distances, it becomes more obvious where there are large numbers of mass or energy entities near each other. (As matter has no pull, the "warping" of space has been proposed in relativity theory.)

If an entity persists long enough in a contracted state, it will eventually be pushed together with other mass. The larger the gathering of mass, the less counteractive space propulsion there is at the center, and therefore the pressure is stronger in that direction according to traditional formulas for gravity. This process is actually an acceleration towards the center, as supported by the equivalence of the formulas for acceleration and gravity. Energy has one-half the gravity of mass. That is, energy is propelled toward mass half the time, during the brief bits when energy is contracted.

The expansive momentum of space entities is $2c$. Since energy is expanded half the time, its waves move at the velocity c. (Einstein's formula, $E = mc^2$, is a simplification of his basic formula which requires the figure $2c$).

The universe is a field of space (any number of space entities) which maintains a constant and uniform pressure on any contracted entities. The pattern of space-energy-mass relations can be applied in modified form to any local context, for instance gas-liquid-solid, or vaporized-fluid-frozen.

The wave-particle duality is simply explained in terms of this concept, since an energy entity is a particle one-half the time. As a wave, the entity is observed in both its space-time and mass-time, since a wave is two changes of state. Perhaps this puzzle was difficult to solve because the wave and the particle are not opposites of each other. Energy has no opposite: it is a combination of opposites. From the perspective of space, energy could be said to be a wave-space duality. It is this oddity of energy that has made it such a tantalizing problem to our reason.

It should be a simple matter to test this concept with computer analysis. The spectrum for any atom can be broken down into the number of unique entities vibrating in given patterns that would be required to produce that spectrum. Every entity in the universe is either on or off, never both at the same time. We could say the universe is a computer in which the 0's and 1's are not fixed, but arbitrarily one or the other at any given time.

The propulsion of mass by space also answers the puzzle of "action at a distance" in gravity. The consciousness of space solves "communication at a distance" by subatomic particles, which leads us to metaphysics.

As for the essential metaphysics of this viewpoint:

If an expanded entity is conscious, and a contracted entity is unconscious, let us see where reason takes us.

Each entity must be either conscious or unconscious at any given instant. When we speak of being "more" or "less" conscious, what we mean is being conscious more or less of the time. Each state is total and absolute.

An energy entity is vibrating, changing states, many millions of times a second. It is conscious therefore in millions of brief bits. These bits are experienced as continuous consciousness, just as we see a film as showing continuous motion, but the entity is actually conscious only half the time. It is aware of only half the information in the local reality.

Similarly, a material entity may subjectively experience its consciousness as continuous, even though it is expanded perhaps only ten percent of the time.

The conscious state is always total, however. The consciousness known by a material entity is exactly the same as that of a space entity, even if it is experienced with different emotions and without the space entity's fullness of conceptualization. Consciousness itself is not the variable: the variable is the time-length of consciousness, as well as the time-proportion of expanded and contracted states in any time period.

We human beings have a poverty of information, just as we would in a crowded room in which the lights flashed on and off once every two seconds, but our consciousness is just as expanded in any instant as it will ever be, during the time-bits we are conscious. We may have little information about the actions of other entities, and may have a distorted perspective, with false assumptions about cause and effect, but such consciousness as we do have is always total.

Our intention, therefore, cannot be to "expand consciousness," but must be to prolong our time-lengths of consciousness, regardless of what we are thinking about. Since the expanded state and consciousness are one and the same, that means that an entity cannot be aware of the actual event of changing states, and of course is not aware of its unconscious phases. No entity can be conscious of what it is itself doing when it is energy or mass. An entity can be aware of the intention to act in a certain way, and will to act in that way, but cannot be conscious of a functional variation while it is happening.

We must thus deal with the peculiar fact that functioning—choosing and changing states—is the essential variable that positions us in a reality, but the behavior itself is not accessible to consciousness. However, we can have objective evidence. We can know what we are doing by the nature of the local reality in which we find ourselves, because like-functioning entities always move into proximity with each other. The local reality we are in is a mirror of our behavior. For if we follow the logic of the law that space propels mass, and therefore that conscious entities propel unconscious entities, we see that all contracting entities must in time move into proximity with others having similar contraction-times.

Once these energy and material entities are near each other, there is a further variation of relations, based on patterns of alternating states. We can see this most clearly in the case of two energy entities, both expanded half the time: if they are unsynchronized, each is always expanded whenever the other is contracted. Each feels the other as an unconscious mass, yet they cannot move away from each other because their time-proportions of contraction are the same. This phenomenon is probably the source of the statement that "opposites attract." It is also the root of persistent pain. All other pains and disagreeable emotions are variations of it. That is why energy realities always hold a potential for persistent pain, and why pain does not persist where there is no energy.

Reality is always an instantaneous universal election. Local realities develop according to the behavior of the basic entities, within the law that space propels mass. No entity can control the behavior of others, and therefore no entity can control a reality or predict its future precisely. Each entity is responsible for its own position in relation to other beings. Each governs only its own functions.

One consequence of these principles is that when an entity prolongs its consciousness, it will inexorably push away all unconsciousness, all energy and mass. A space entity cannot continue a relation with any given energy or mass entities, though it may, if it chooses, wander through accumulations of energy or mass without impedance.

Energy has more consciousness-time than matter, but it is not necessary for any entity to go through a stage of being energy when it chooses to be space. An entity that has been contracted and unconscious for eons can instantly change to a conscious state and maintain it continuously. Such an entity might awaken in the middle of a strange planet or star, since we awaken where we have been sleeping, but nothing can prevent it from moving back to a space reality.

All entities move closer in time to others of similar behavior. Energy entities, however, must always synchronize vibrations with neighbors, in order to avoid the pain of functional difference in proximity. It is only in energy realities that pain can persist, and fortunately we are not obliged to be energy.

The maximum consciousness and the easiest functional agreement occurs among entities that are expanded all the time. When we are space, we have the maximum freedom of position and momentum, and complete freedom to be aware of any concepts at all. We can forget about this book.

Post-Script

I wrote *The Lazy Man's Guide to Enlightenment* in language that any reader of English could understand, making it as easy as possible. Now, in writing *Love and Pain*, I decided to state the case as clearly as I could without regard to a general audience, as though I was writing to a friend, someone like myself. I knew I was a man in the middle in a number of ways.

As the child of immigrants, I had few roots in American culture, but I was clever enough to get a good university education. I still felt as much European as American. My concepts were not academically respectable, indeed they were alien to the canons of science, and at the same time *Love and Pain* would repel almost everyone in the New Age mind-set.

But I now had the key to our systems-reality: Power begins with the willingness to endure pain without changing. Everyone wants power. Even the New Age people want the world to bend to their thoughts. If *Love and Pain* proves to be practical, practicality will make it popular enough.

More than that, I have no expectation that the book will produce any beneficial consequence in human existence.

The laws that govern the behavior of energy and the interactions of material systems cannot be contradicted. I have no wish to convert people, therefore. I know what I need to know to go where I want to go, and I have made the information available to others if they want it. Others are free to do as they will, and I am free to relate to them or not.

There are, however, great advantages in the information in this book: knowing how our reality works, we can avoid wasting emotions, time and effort in pursuit of false goals. Personally, I found great relief in realizing that I was not obliged to correct anyone's erroneous opinions, since ideas do not do anything.

Also, I could stop criticizing myself for failing to dwell in constant bliss. When I encounter pain, it does not mean that I have necessarily been stupid: pain is inevitable in human life, whichever path we take.

Neither am I obliged to rescue others from their pain: they will gain greater strength in enduring it and solving their own difficulties. That which offends the sentimental in the short run is often the greatest kindness over a longer time. I try to be kind to strong people because they have endured much to become strong.

I know there are enormous industries built on the flight from pain. The cost of medical care multiplies much faster than the rate of inflation, and the children of the middle class inherit little wealth. A better understanding of the role of pain in our lives might diminish such nonsense, but the net quotient of suffering will probably remain the same.

I am not offering that sort of deliverance.

What I do offer in *Love and Pain* is a clear understanding of the real benefits that any person may expect from prolonging consciousness.

Consciousness does not give the power to control energy and matter. It is the power to push them away, to leave this reality and stay away. That is all consciousness does, but it is enough. The rewards are truly much more profound than anything we can enjoy on Earth.

In essence, I suppose I am saying: You can leave and go to heaven. Here is how to do it, but I cannot care whether you do it or not. Meanwhile, human life will always have its inevitable difficulties. If we do not take the pain of cooperation and of postponed gratification, we will suffer disorder. I know this is not a particularly inspiring message, but it is the reality we will always collide with as human beings. I cannot imagine what a society would be like in which all people acted on such information. I do not intend to look back to find out. I have solved the problem to my own satisfaction and have no further interest in figuring it out.

I am older now, and perhaps weary with the effort of exploring false trails and persisting until I found better ones. When my first book was published, I considered it was sufficient to read the first line of Chapter One: "We are equal beings and the universe is our relations with each other."

Once that idea was installed in the mental computer, I thought, any mind could sort itself out. Perhaps others can give it better extension than I have.

And now, knowing we must all go where no baggage can be taken, at least little more than a simple idea, I would suggest again the simplest of intentions:

No matter what happens I am conscious all the time.

The AUTHOR

Thaddeus Golas was a witness to the 20th century's great upheavals.

Born in 1924 in Paterson, New Jersey, to Polish Catholic parents, he was a child of Einstein's Relativity but also of the Great Depression.

He served a long European tour of duty in WWII, and was in Patton's Third Army in Antwerp, but narrowly avoided combat at the Battle of the Bulge. The G.I. Bill helped him earn a BA in General Humanities from New York's Columbia University where he studied under Jacques Barzun, among notable others.

He went on to work as a proofreader for Betty Ballantine, as a book editor for Redbook, and later, in Oklahoma, as a sales representative for Harper & Row. He saw the rise of the Beat Movement in Manhattan, with its onset of mind-altering substances.

His ideas on human consciousness had gathered over many years of pondering Eastern Mysticism and popular Quantum Science; when he moved to California in the '60s, he was encouraged by Alan Watts, Timothy Leary, and former high school mate Allen Ginsberg to self-publish his first effort: *The Lazy Man's Guide to Enlightenment*. Thus, it was in the psychedelic maelstrom, in the midst of San Francisco's Haight-Ashbury turmoil at the start of the Seventies, that Thaddeus Golas achieved recognition as a major philosopher. He stood on street corners with his third wife Nancy Monroe, come rain or come shine, selling copies to passersby to make ends meet. *The Lazy Man's Guide to Enlightenment* caught-on like wild fire, and Golas, the reluctant guru, became a bit of a sensation. His book remained in print for nearly 40 years and was translated into seven languages.

Often shunned by members of the New Age community for his biting criticism of their manipulations, Thaddeus Golas remained a nomad and led a discreet life, declining to lecture or exploit his readers with seminars. He continued to write throughout the Eighties and Nineties, but never managed to publish again, save for a few articles.

Love and Pain, his new book, is published some twenty years after it was completed. *The Cosmic Airdrome*, *Pocket Physics*, and his biography: *The Lazy Man's Life* are also published posthumously.

Thaddeus Golas married and divorced three times.

A lifelong smoker, he died of pneumonia in Sarasota, Florida, in the spring of 1997.

ALSO AVAILABLE
by Thaddeus Golas
from SEED CENTER BOOKS:

The Lazy Man's Guide to Enlightenment — A Young Person's Guide Edition (Updated and revised by author Thaddeus Golas.)

The Lazy Man's Guide to Enlightenment — The Audio CD. (Spoken Word, Read, and Revised by author Thaddeus Golas.)

The Cosmic Airdrome — Aphorisms and flights of fancy into Space Consciousness.

The Lazy Man's Life — The Life and Times of Thaddeus Golas. (Autobiography of Thaddeus Golas.)

FORTHCOMING:
Pocket Physics — Writings, Articles, Interviews and Essays.

Tired of turning the pages?

BECOME **EVEN LAZIER:**

You've read the book,
now sit back,
and let Thaddeus Golas read
The Lazy Man's Guide to Enlightenment to you,
in the comfort of your home, car, or hammock!
Order your double AUDIO CD from our website
and experience the *Guide* in the voice of its author.
This digital 'spoken word' edition of
The Lazy Man's Guide to Enlightenment comes with its
own 22-page booklet of revisions and pointers
also written by Thaddeus Golas.
Rediscover this unique and legendary book
through the voice of Thaddeus Golas.

Find it at:
www.seedcenterbooks.com

For more information about Thaddeus Golas *visit*:
www.thaddeusgolas.com

Printed in Sofia, Bulgaria
on the presses of Tezida Ltd.